Counseling Lesbian Partners

Counseling and Pastoral Theology

Andrew D. Lester, Series Editor

Counseling Lesbian Partners

Joretta L. Marshall

Westminster John Knox Press
Louisville, Kentucky

Book design by Jennifer K. Cox
Series cover design by Kevin Darst

First edition
Published by Westminster John Knox Press
Louisville, Kentucky

This book is printed on acid-free paper that meets the
American National Standards Institute Z39.48 standard. ♾

PRINTED IN THE UNITED STATES OF AMERICA
97 98 99 00 01 02 03 04 05 06 — 10 9 8 7 6 5 4 3 2 1

Library of Congress Cataloging-in-Publication Data

Marshall, Joretta L.
    Counseling lesbian partners / Joretta L. Marshall. — 1st ed.
        p.   cm. — (Counseling and pastoral theology)
    Includes bibliographical references and index.
    ISBN 0-664-25532-9 (alk. paper)
    1. Lesbian couples—Pastoral counseling of.   I. Title.
II. Series.
BV4437.5.M37   1997
259'.08'6643—dc20   96-44113

To Joy S. Allen

Contents

Foreword

Given the ambivalence the church has expressed toward homosexual men and women, it is not surprising that many hesitate to bring their relationship problems to pastoral care professionals. Yet many pastoral care specialists are privileged to minister with gay men and lesbian women whose partnerships are stressed. As the author notes, this book is written for "those who want to provide sensitive and appropriate care to women in lesbian relationships." Jorètta Marshall gives specific guidance to those who are uncertain of their own internal response to lesbian women, leading them through exercises that enable self-reflection. Furthermore, she carefully confronts the theological questions and gives a reasoned, biblical response.

Lesbian relationships are vulnerable to many of the same stresses that plague heterosexual relationships. Marshall chooses to explore the effect of addictions, violence, emotional fusion, and early sexual abuse. Even when the issues are similar, however, unique factors contribute to the struggles experienced within lesbian relationships. The dynamics of establishing a clear lesbian identity, the "coming out" process, and the struggles of relating to extended families are two examples she explores in depth. If the pastoral care specialist is to offer a response which enables women partners to experience the presence and grace of God in their lives, then learning about these unique dynamics is imperative.

Given the absence of cultural rituals that support and affirm their relationships, lesbian women must look to a deeper core of truth for guidance in nurturing and strengthening their partnerships. In response, Professor Marshall offers a pastoral theological understanding of the nature of relationships that focuses on covenants. She offers guidance for "pastoral representatives who bring the resources of pastoral theology to the experiences of women partners [and] provide sanctuaries" in which women in lesbian relationships can develop "convenantal partnerships based upon love, justice, and mutuality." The case studies in each chapter enable the reader to consider how the pastoral theology constructed by Professor Marshall informs both assessment and intervention.

I am grateful to Joretta for taking the personal risk inherent in writing this book. Her experience living within a convenantal relationship with her partner for fifteen years enhances our learning. She consulted with clients, colleagues, friends, and students who are lesbian women so that the reader benefits from a book written by one who knows the issues clinically, academically, and experientially.

The *Counseling and Pastoral Theology* Series

The purpose of this series is to address clinical issues that arise among particular populations currently neglected in the literature on pastoral care and counseling (women in lesbian relationships, African American couples, adolescents under stress, women who are depressed, survivors of sexual abuse, adult adoptees, persons with terminal illness, and couples experiencing infertility). This series is committed to enhancing both the theoretical base and the clinical expertise of pastoral caregivers by providing a pastoral theological paradigm that will inform both assessment and intervention with persons in these specific populations.

Many books in pastoral care and counseling are more carefully informed by the behavioral and social sciences than by classical theological disciplines. Pastoral care and counseling specialists have been criticized for ignoring our theological heritage, challenged to reevaluate our idolization of psychology, and to claim our unique perspectives on the human predicament. The discipline of pastoral theology has made significant strides in the last decade. The Society for Pastoral Theology was formed in 1985 and now publishes *The Journal of Pastoral Theology*.

Pastoral theology grows out of data gathered from at least three sources: (1) revelation about the human condition uncovered by the social and behavioral sciences, (2) wisdom from the classical theological disciplines, and (3) insight garnered from reflection on the pastoral ministry event. The development of pastoral theology grows out of the dialogue among these three perspectives, each perspective enabled to ask questions of, challenge, and critique the other perspectives.

Each author is clinically experienced and academically prepared to write about the particular population with which she or he is personally concerned and professionally involved. Each author develops a "constructive pastoral theology," resulting in the theological frame of reference that provides the unique perspective from which a pastoral person approaches both assessment and intervention. This constructive pastoral theology will enable clinically trained pastors and pastoral care specialists (pastoral counselors, chaplains, Clinical Pastoral Education supervisors) to creatively participate in pastoral relationships that effectively enable healing, sustaining, guiding, reconciling, and liberating.

Though the focus will be on offering pastoral care and counseling to individuals, couples, and families, each author is cognizant of the interaction between individuals and their environment. These books will consider the effects of larger systems—from family of origin to cultural constructs. Each author will use case material from her or his clinical pastoral ministry which will serve to focus the reader's attention on the issues faced by the particular population as viewed from the pastoral theological paradigm.

My thanks to colleagues who faithfully served on the Advisory Committee and spent many hours in creative work to ensure that this series would make a substantial contribution: Bonnie Miller-McLemore (1992–96), Nancy Ramsay (1992–96), Han van den Blink (1992–94), Larry Graham (1994–96), Linda Kirkland-Harris (1994–96).

Andrew D. Lester
Brite Divinity School

Preface

Women in lesbian relationships have much to lose and much to gain by confiding in pastoral care specialists. Those who represent the church have not always affirmed the lives of women who openly share their love for other women. Previous experiences in the church that have left women feeling unwanted or dismissed make it difficult for them to approach pastoral care specialists. Women have much to lose as they seek support, realizing through experience and intuition that not every pastoral representative can affirm the presence and grace of God in their lives as women who love women.

Yet women in lesbian relationships have much to gain as they are met by pastoral care specialists who respond to their stories with passion and compassion. Pastoral representatives who bring the resources of pastoral theology to the experiences of women partners provide sanctuaries as women reflect on their lives with new meaning. Women struggling in their relationships have much to gain as they find caregivers who assist them in developing covenantal partnerships based upon love, justice, and mutuality.

Pastoral caregivers also have much to gain by working with women in lesbian relationships. The experiences of these women offer insights into issues of pastoral theology, justice and power, sexuality, and spirituality. Those who affirm women in lesbian partnerships can be proactive in their ministries, not only by responding when women approach them for care but by becoming more visible in the community as they work for justice. Pastoral care specialists may also raise their prophetic voices in church structures as they speak about the concerns of lesbians, gay men, and bisexuals.

Pastoral caregivers must also come to terms with what they have to lose by working with women in lesbian partnerships. People who are not supportive of pastoral care specialists who affirm women in lesbian partnerships may withdraw their financial support or referral base. Yet countless others—women and men in partnerships, parents and siblings of lesbians and gay men, communities of faith—will experience grace as pastoral caregivers risk offering their prophetic witness and pastoral response to the concerns raised in this book. To be proactive means more than affirming women in lesbian relationships. Rather, proactivity suggests that pastoral care specialists intentionally take the initiative and the inevitable risk of openly voicing their support and affirmation of women in lesbian partnerships, knowing that professionally they have something to lose but trusting that there is much more to be gained.

This book is written to challenge pastoral care specialists to be proactive in their ministries with women in lesbian relationships. In what follows the focus is on lesbian relationships and partnerships rather than on individual issues in the counseling process. Many issues are touched upon too briefly, but must be left for others to explore in depth in some other format.

The majority of those who read this book will do so because they are interested in offering pastoral care to women in lesbian relationships but are not lesbians themselves. What follows is an attempt to present some of the dynamics present in women's relationships with one another. For some this book may seem too radical because it assumes that women in lesbian relationships are to be affirmed and invited to develop faithful covenants with each other built on the qualities of love, justice, and mutuality. For others it will seem too traditional because it is grounded in a Judeo-Christian perspective of covenants and partnerships, or too limited because it does not resolve the underlying philosophical and theological tensions that surface in its pages.

This book offers a pastoral theological perspective for those who want to provide sensitive and appropriate care to women in lesbian relationships. The first chapter explores the assumptions that ground this work, along with discussions about the interpretations of scripture, moral issues, and the roles of sexism and heterosexism in pastoral care. The process of identity formation for women who self-identify as lesbian is covered in the second chapter. In chapter 3 the focus shifts to covenantal lesbian partnerships as places where love, justice, and mutuality are embodied. The fourth chapter addresses four common obstacles to relationships that may appear in counseling with women partners. Chapter 5 deals with coming out, particularly in the context of families of origin and the creation of lesbian families of choice. The final chapter challenges pastoral care specialists to become proactive in their ministries with women in lesbian relationships.

I have tried to be clear about the broader communal and ecclesial issues that are at stake for those of us who live at the margins of the church and of the culture. In being proactive I bring my own experience to this project as a woman who carries the pains, fears, and hopes of knowing that in writing this book I have much to gain and much to lose. My fears and hopes parallel the fears and hopes that women in lesbian partnerships bring to the pastoral care context. Sharing the secrets of our lives, the vulnerabilities of our loves, and the burdens of our families places us in the precarious position of experiencing rejection and intolerance, or liberation and transformation.

In spite of my fears I trust that this book will be met with the same kind of respect, openness, and care expressed by many colleagues, peers, and friends during its preparation. As in every writing endeavor, a book represents not just one person's perspective, but also the professional support of many others: Andy Lester, who initially invited me to work on this project and who has remained steadfast in working with me; Larry Graham, who has maintained a collegial presence, offering invaluable conversation and being compassionately present as I struggled with the task of writing; Kathleen Greider, Gordon Kieft, Victor Nelson, and Christie Neuger, who read the manuscript and offered helpful suggestions; Nancy Ramsay, who has become a conversation partner and friend; colleagues at Vanderbilt Divinity School, where this book first took shape, and at Iliff School of Theology, where it was completed; clients who have shared their life journeys and their lesbian partnerships; supervisors and colleagues at the Pastoral Care and Counseling Centers of Tennessee in Nashville who participated in my clinical development; students at Vanderbilt and Iliff who read pieces of the manuscript and offered insightful comments, particularly the lesbian students at Vanderbilt Divinity School, with whom I had numerous conversations; research assistants Anne McWilliams and Jeanne Hoeft and especially Sharyl Peterson, who worked on editing and reading this book several times during its process.

At a more personal level there are many who have persevered with me in struggling to bring this book to life: my parents, sister, and extended family who continue to love me in the midst of their own fears about my openness; Cindy Woods, who continues to be part of my family; a women's potluck group in Nashville; and countless friends who have nurtured me in ways too numerous to mention and who are loved more deeply than they will ever realize. Finally, Joy Allen has offered her daily presence, her challenge to remain centered in the spiritual journey, and her gifts of encouragement and care. With her I continue to learn about living in a dynamic covenantal partnership of love, justice, and mutuality.

Joretta L. Marshall

Denver, Colorado

Chapter One

Pastoral Counseling and Women in Lesbian Relationships

Mary makes an appointment with a pastoral caregiver whom she does not know.[1] She begins the session tentatively, suggesting that there are "spiritual and relational issues" she wants to discuss with the pastor. All at once the conversation turns into a series of questions directed at the caregiver: "What church do you belong to? Would you define yourself as liberal or conservative? How do you interpret the scriptures? What do you think about homosexuality—is it a sin or is it normal?"

Initially the pastoral care specialist feels somewhat defensive about these inquiries into his belief system. However, respecting Mary's questions, the caregiver responds in a succinct and careful manner. Mary reveals that she is involved in a primary relationship with another woman. She grew up in a church that does not accept homosexuality and she is confused about her feelings. She called a pastoral care specialist because she wants help in sorting through the questions about her faith, her spirituality, and her sexuality.

Will she be condemned as she was by her mother's pastor, who said he would pray for her to find a good husband to help her? Or will she be patronized and told that she is "going through a phase"? Or will Mary be met in this situation by a pastoral care specialist who can hear her pain and confusion, accepting her and working with her to make sense of her sexual feelings?

Mary's story reflects the need for a pastoral perspective when working with women in lesbian relationships. Pastoral care specialists have many opportunities to walk on sacred ground with persons who are seeking to bring meaning and coherence to their life stories. At a deeper symbolic level, pastoral caregivers serve to remind persons of the steadfast presence of God as they embody the presence of a Being who actively works for justice, grace, and compassion in the world. Women who love women approach pastoral persons hoping to be met by caregivers who understand the complexities of integrating their sexual identities, spiritual lives, and relational experiences in the context of often painful messages sent by the church and the society.

To put the issues of lesbian relationships into a pastoral theological perspective, we begin with a discussion of the moral controversy surrounding homosexuality and of several moral options for understanding homosexuality that are available to pastoral caregivers.

Homosexuality as a Moral Issue

The pastoral care relationship provides a sacred space for women to reflect theologically and spiritually on their lives and relationships. For some women, theological and moral questions about orientation emerge as they discover their feelings for other women or as they make choices about a particular relationship. Women who are very comfortable with self-identifying as lesbians request pastoral care as they are confronted by questions from families, local congregations, denominational structures, legal systems, or in other public realms. Effective pastoral care specialists offer women in lesbian relationships the sacred space needed to reflect upon their lives together as well as upon the confusion and fragmentation of the culture in which they live.

Mary and her partner raise questions that have become part of intense moral debates in mainline denominations, local churches, communities, and families. Pastoral leaders carry the unique responsibility for attending to the experiences of women such as Mary and placing them within the broader framework of the church. Although caregivers cannot speak for lesbians, we can earnestly listen to the stories of despair, pain, rejection, and hope from women and their families. As a result, pastoral care specialists can empower silent or quiet voices to speak and to be heard in congregational and denominational debates. There are also times when pastoral representatives can become spokespersons on behalf of those who cannot speak for themselves.

To serve women in lesbian relationships, a pastoral caregiver needs to consider honestly her or his own stance toward homosexuality. Such moral and theological deliberations should include the interpretations the caregiver brings to scriptures and the denominational position, scientific or theoretical perspectives, and the lived experiences of women in relationships with one another. Pastoral care specialists reflecting upon their own perspectives may find it helpful to consider a model suggested by Patricia Jung and Ralph Smith, who identify five moral positions held with respect to homosexuality. The positions separate sexual orientations from sexual behavior.[2] Homosexual orientations are understood to be the internal attractions persons have for those of the same sex, while homosexual behavior refers to explicit sexual expressions between persons of the same sex. The positions recognize that people distinguish between sexual orientations and behaviors as they make their judgments about homosexuality.

The first of Jung and Smith's moral positions is that "[h]omosexual orientations are unnatural; just, loving, and faithful homosexual behavior is evil."[3] From this perspective both orientation and behavior are condemned as immoral or sinful. Women are neither genetically predisposed nor normally attracted to persons of the same sex. Counselors who adopt this position advocate "change," "reparative," or "transformation" therapy.[4] The goal of pastoral counseling from this perspective is to encourage women away from their sin and into heterosexual relationships.

The second moral position claims that "[h]omosexual orientations are diseased; just, loving, and faithful homosexual behavior is not justified."[5] This interpretation of both orientation and behavior as being pathological is analogous to the disease concept of alcoholism.

> Since advocates of this position believe no cure exists for the underlying condition and that no one is able to choose this sexual orientation apart from a physiological predisposition, they attach little to no moral blame to being homosexual in orientation. Homosexuality is a disorder, not primarily a sin. . . . The analogy with alcoholism is clear; it is a sin only when one does not take up the struggle to control it.[6]

From this position women may not have control over their orientations, but they do have responsibility for their behavior. Because "homosexuality is incurable and destructive," same-sex relationships cannot be defended.[7] Pastoral care specialists who align themselves with this approach often encourage sexual abstinence.[8]

A third moral position outlined by Jung and Smith argues that "[h]omosexual orientations are defective; some just, loving, and faithful homosexual behavior may be permissible."[9] From this perspective, women do not make choices about being created as lesbians, but there is something "defective" or "abnormal" about being attracted to other women. This perspective appears to be morally neutral since some lesbian partnerships can be interpreted as providing the best possible option for persons who are created with this abnormality. Pastoral caregivers who hold this position encourage "closeted" living for lesbians, focusing on ways women can adapt in a healthy manner to their abnormal condition.[10]

The fourth moral position asserts that "[h]omosexual orientations are imperfect; just, loving, and faithful homosexual behavior is justified."[11] While lesbian relationships are not to be seen as normative, they are justifiable for those who are homosexual. This stance is slightly more affirming than the previous position in that it allows for a qualified acceptance of homosexual relationships. Those who advocate this moral perspective often acknowledge that lesbians and their relationships should be protected under the principles of human rights. Pastoral caregivers operating from this belief may embrace women who love women while at the same time interpreting their orientation to be the result of arrested development or some other internal psychic mechanism beyond their control.

The final position articulated by Jung and Smith is that "[h]omosexual orientations are natural; just, loving, and faithful homosexual behavior is good."[12] Caregivers operating from this stance not only affirm lesbian women as being normal, but also embrace lesbian orientation as "a natural variation in the created order."[13] In its strongest vein this perspective claims that women who are lesbian in orientation are blessed by the creation of their sexual feelings and attractions and are not defective or lacking in any way. Covenantal lesbian partnerships should be created, nurtured, and maintained. It is from this perspective that this book is written.

The typology outlined by Jung and Smith is helpful to pastoral care specialists in at least three ways. First, it explicitly separates homosexual orientation from same-gender sexual behavior. Orientation and behavior are interdependent, yet they are not identical. Not all women who have participated in some level of sexual activity with other women self-identify as lesbian. Similarly, not all women who are physically and sexually attracted to women choose lesbian relationships. How pastoral caregivers interpret internal orientations—whether they are matters of choice, learned behaviors, or genetic predispositions—guides how they respond to lesbian partnerships.

Second, the typology of Jung and Smith can be helpful as pastoral caregivers assess their own positions. Clients and parishioners are most helped when caregivers are not caught in their own moral struggles at the same moment in which they are trying to assist women, their partners, their families, or their congregations. Most women would rather engage in honest deliberation with pastoral caregivers who bring clarity to their praxis but with whom they may disagree than to be met by care specialists who are uncertain about their own stances.

Finally, this typology is beneficial because it offers a framework for understanding where particular clients, partnerships, families, or churches stand in respect to their moral beliefs about homosexual orientations and behavior. To have a typology from which to work can assist caregivers in discerning how to intervene with persons. Although it is not the task of pastoral representatives to convince persons to shift from one position to another, it is important to know when to challenge positions and when to refer persons to other caregivers who may be more in line with the perspectives of the parishioner or client.

Many women in lesbian relationships, their extended families, and their faith communities ask about particular biblical passages as they sort out their moral perspective. Scripture has often been used to condemn homosexual orientations and behavior, viewing them as sins, perversions, unnatural, or indicative of psychic illness. Scholars disagree when it comes to interpreting scriptures, and it is not the purpose of this book to repeat the studies others have pursued in detail and with rigor.[14] However, those portions of the Bible that are construed as prohibitions against homosexual behavior (since orientation is rarely alluded to in the Bible) are important to consider.

Pastoral specialists need not shy away from talking about scripture with lesbian clients or their families. Caregivers can participate in liberating scriptures from the shackles that sometimes constrict and distort them. The approaches parishioners and clients bring to the interpretation of all scripture, not only the texts that have been said to pertain to homosexuality, provide insight into their use of the Bible. Beginning conversations by looking at passages other than those related to homosexuality may be helpful. For example, asking parishioners or clients about their interpretation of Paul's discussion on women or on marriage, or what characters in the Bible they identify with most, can establish a context for talking about the importance and role of scripture.

A deliberate approach to biblical texts by the caregiver signals to parishioners and clients a willingness to wrestle with slippery issues and to remain open to new interpretations.[15] Jung and Smith suggest that a liberating question such as the following can be brought to the scriptures: "Are the traditional heterosexist interpretations of these biblical texts ultimately death dealing or life giving to gay and lesbian Christians?"[16] Against this backdrop the pastoral nature of care becomes quite explicit.

When working with scriptures and women who are in same-sex relationships, it is crucial to remember that the cultural context out of which the biblical tradition comes is primarily patriarchal. The Bible speaks little about women and only once about women who love women.[17] Robin Scroggs, author of *The New Testament and Homosexuality*, suggests this lack of attention to women in relationship with one another reflects the fact that "[e]ither the male author had no interest in such relationships or no knowledge about it or . . . he avoided it because it was a threat to the male ego. How could women like women more than they liked men?"[18] Most scholars have come to recognize that scripture must be understood in the context of this patriarchal structure.

In a similar manner, the word *homosexual* never appears in the original language of the scriptures. The term was brought into usage in the late 1800s.[19] Hence, all references to homosexuality in scripture are inferred rather than made in direct statements. While many scriptures pertain to the nature of relating to one another with a sense of love and respect—with eros and agape love—four sets of texts have become central to the arguments about homosexuality. Pastoral caregivers need to have a clear grasp of the scriptures in order to offer thoughtful interpretations for the creation stories in Genesis, the story of the community of Sodom (Gen. 19:1–29), the Holiness Code of Leviticus (Lev. 18:22; 20:13), and the passages from the New Testament (Rom. 1:18–32; 1 Cor. 6:9–11; 1 Tim. 1:8–11). Research continues to offer insights into these scriptures, and pastoral caregivers who seek to assist parishioners and clients should continue to be informed by such writings.

The commonality in all the scriptures is their condemnation of actions that exhibit sexualized violence or abuse. Women who love women are not the objects of anxiety; rather, what troubles the writers of scripture are relationships that use sexuality in a derogatory, demeaning, or dehumanizing manner. All relationships, whether they are heterosexual, lesbian, or gay, are encouraged in the scriptures to have as their foundation the qualities that lead to right relationships with self, others, and God.

Pastoral caregivers can help parishioners find illumination by recognizing the stories within scripture that reflect genuine love and care between persons of the same sex. For example, the stories of Jonathan and David and of Ruth and Naomi tell of persons of the same sex who share deep caring and respect. While it may not be said that these relationships are illustrative of "same-sex" orientation, they do exhort the beauty of friendships and relationships that claim love, justice, and mutuality as the core way of relating.[20] The power of the Bible rests in the ability of pastoral care specialists, parishioners, churches, and clients to listen carefully for the liberating activity of God. Drawing upon various stories, not only those discussed above, leads to conversations about what it means to be in right relationship with one another.

Sexism and Heterosexism

Lesbians contend with the social, cultural, and religious structures of patriarchy. There has been considerable analysis of the detrimental effect patriarchal religion has had on women in general.[21] Gender discrimination, particularly in the forms of sexism and heterosexism, has a unique impact upon lesbian relationships and, in turn, upon the pastoral care lesbians receive.[22]

While a more systematic look at gender and identity formation appears in chapter 2, a working definition is useful at this point for contemplating how sexism is experienced by women in lesbian partnerships. In their text *Feminist Perspectives in Therapy: An Empowerment Model for Women*, therapists Judith Worell and Pam Remer define gender as one of the most salient categories by which people judge and evaluate others. . . . We define *gender* as culturally-determined cognitions, attitudes, and belief systems about females and males. Gender is a concept that varies across cultures, that changes through historical time, and that differs in terms of who makes the observations and judgments.[23]

Forces that contribute to the social construction of gender include patriarchy, economic structures, sexism, racism, feminism, psychological processes, and life development events.[24] In addition, religious and theological assumptions communicate beliefs about gender and sexuality.

Sexism

Sexism refers to the forms of systematic and structural oppression operative in the culture that deny women power or recognition. Pastoral care specialists need to work assertively in identifying sexism when it appears in the culture and, even more importantly, in the office of the caregiver. Feminist theory can assist in this process as it "challenges us to recognize the need to investigate carefully what is at the surface, and what is at the core of beliefs, symbols, assumptions, and categories of meaning-making."[25] Biases about gender and sexuality on the part of the caregiver can be injurious to women in lesbian relationships.

Worell and Remer propose three feminist principles that can assist pastoral caregivers.[26] The first principle, "the personal is political," connects individual care and counseling with the politics of gender and sexism. Issues of diagnosis, intervention, and interpretations are always to be understood against the broader sociopolitical context of the culture. For example, women who exhibit intense fear about being "discovered" as lesbians are sometimes dismissed as being paranoid, characterological, or too enmeshed with their families of origin. However, hesitancy about being openly lesbian can be viewed as a healthy, self-protective way for women to live in light of the risks they face: losing jobs, families, and friends. Pastoral caregivers can openly discuss this tension with parishioners and clients as a way of connecting personal and political realities.

Not only personal issues but theological understandings are related to political concerns, and both can be used negatively against women.[27] Lesbians usually are not told that they are gifts in God's creation. The perpetual silence on the part of pastoral caregivers about homosexuality is as destructive to lesbians as is the proclamation of those who condemn. Having heard the personal stories of women in lesbian relationships, pastoral care specialists carry an increased responsibility to challenge theological assertions that are destructive rather than liberating. Constructing pastoral theological statements from the vantage point of lesbians can contribute to the redemptive process of liberation for all persons.

A second principle of feminist therapy outlined by Worell and Remer is the belief that "interpersonal relationships should be as egalitarian as possible."[28] Pastoral care specialists often intervene in relationships where mutuality and egalitarianism are far from the reality. The third chapter of this book examines how the theological image of covenant embodies the qualities of love, justice, and mutuality in lesbian relationships. Assisting women to live in this kind of covenantal partnership encourages the building of relationships that are based on mutual and egalitarian principles.

Power is a dynamic that is present in all relationships. When used perversely or abusively power prevents women from being mutual and egalitarian with one another. Women in lesbian relationships struggle with the dynamics of power in ways that are indicative of the gender structures they bring to their relationships. Questions about who controls the checkbook and the money, who has major responsibility for the care of the children, and how decisions that affect both persons are made, become part of the context of care.[29] Power, of course, is also present as pastoral caregivers choose the theories and theologies that guide their interpretations and interventions. Recognizing the presence of power in pastoral care situations—and the potential for abusing power—continues to be imperative for those lesbian partners who approach representatives of the church.

Worell and Remer's third principle is that of valuing the female perspective.[30] Working with women in lesbian relationships means taking seriously the perspectives each woman brings as a female. An assumption is often made that two women will bring the same perspective since both are female. This, however, is not necessarily the case. Another bias caregivers sometimes have emerges in the assumption that one of the women of a partnership should act more like a traditional male while the other takes the role of a traditional female. Women who are not traditionally feminine in their dress and mannerisms should not be labeled as "tomboyish" or gender dystonic. The aim of good pastoral care is to celebrate how each person brings her own unique gifts and qualities as a woman into the partnership.

An awareness of potentially sexist biases on the part of the pastoral caregiver must be matched by a willingness to confront intentionally those structures in the church, in theology, and in the culture which denigrate women.

Heterosexism

As a culture we have become somewhat accustomed to addressing critically the presence of patriarchy and sexism.[31] The presence of heterosexism, however, has not been as carefully or consistently drawn to the attention of the pastoral care community. Heterosexism is the systemic, structural, and often unconscious legitimation of traditional relationships between men and women in ways detrimental to women in lesbian relationships and to gay men. The structures that foster heterosexism are connected intimately to structures that support sexism.[32]

Legal privileges, marital status, and even pastoral care are offered to traditional families at the expense of those who are single, divorced, widowed, or in lesbian or gay relationships. For example, traditional marriages between men and women are understood to be normative and healthy in North American culture. Those who are single, however, are thought to be missing out on something important in life and are unconsciously viewed as being less than whole persons. Women who appear to be single may experience the reality of both sexism and heterosexism.

Heterosexual privilege—the implicit structures and assumptions that support couples in traditional heterosexual relationships and marriages—is so common that pastoral caregivers may be unaware of its power and presence. Some illustrations help show how heterosexual privilege appears in everyday reality. Holding the hand of someone of the opposite sex in public is understood as a sign of affection and love and is generally affirmed by others. However, two women who hold hands usually encounter raised eyebrows, verbal scorn, or disbelief on the part of others. Many lesbians never experience the privilege of openly expressing affection for the person they love in a public place without fearing the response of others.

Another example of heterosexual privilege is reflected in the social structures that support male-female couples in legal or financial ways. Health insurance is usually offered to traditionally married partners and their families but rarely extended to those not considered to be legally married. Many lesbians and their children must secure health care coverage at higher financial costs than can legally married couples. Likewise, there is an implicit understanding that husbands and wives can make some decisions about health care for each other in the midst of crises. In contrast, the "next of kin" is rarely the lesbian partner but more often a blood relative who may or may not be close to the woman involved in the crisis.

Heterosexism is also present in the pastoral care context. Intake forms for pastoral counseling centers often ask for the spouse's, husband's, or wife's name. Rarely are women in lesbian relationships given the opportunity to designate a "significant other" or "life partner." Instead, persons are assumed to be single if they do not list a designated wife or husband on the form. Women in lesbian partnerships are not always understood to be a "couple" even by therapists who work out of systems or family models.

Homophobia is a word often used in connection with heterosexism. The latter term reflects the cultural and systemic structures that support heterosexual couples, while homophobia refers to internalized feelings. Homophobia is the internal fear of being assumed to be lesbian or gay, or disgust at persons who are in same-sex relationships, or uncomfortableness in the presence of persons of the same sex. Even pastoral caregivers who claim they are minimally homophobic may perpetuate structures that offer more support to traditional male-female relationships than to lesbian partnerships. Lesbians may also experience internalized homophobia when they think there is something "wrong" with being attracted to other women, or when they feel that they don't deserve the same privileges as are granted to those in heterosexual relationships.

Heterosexism and homophobia prevent all women and men from participating fully in the life of the community of faith. Institutional and systemic injustice are sins that hinder lesbians from affirming their value and worth. Pastoral care specialists are called to be keenly aware of internalized homophobia and heterosexual privilege in their praxis.

Responding to Mary

Mary's story, at the beginning of this chapter, provides a context for reflecting upon pastoral care with women in lesbian relationships. Mary has called a pastoral care specialist whom she does not know. Her anxiety about the process, her concerns about the openness of this person to her lesbian orientation, and her awareness of the heterosexist biases of the church and the culture make it understandable that Mary would begin her conversation with a series of questions. She is not being reactive or manipulative; she simply needs to know where the caregiver stands before she can be open and honest. In this case the pastoral care specialist responded by giving information that put Mary at ease. Being direct, open, and honest is imperative when creating nonsexist and nonheterosexist environments.

Some pastoral caregivers dismiss the anxiety of lesbians as being no more intense than that of others who enter the counseling office. While at one level this may be true, to assume that lesbians do not carry additional anxiety because of theological and cultural biases is to deny Mary's reality. Most likely Mary has to decide daily who to trust, how to share her lesbian orientation with others, and how to deal with those who deny her worth as a lesbian woman. Being lesbian is about a core self-understanding, and Mary is acutely aware that revealing her orientation to a pastoral caregiver could result in an experience of damaging condemnation rather than openness and acceptance.

Pastoral caregivers can confront the heterosexism present in the culture by not immediately assuming that women are either lesbian or straight. Listening carefully to the language Mary uses to talk about herself and the person she loves can provide the specialist with a sense of how Mary makes meaning of her orientation and her partnership. Inviting Mary's partner into the counseling process is appropriate. A pastoral representative who affirms them as partners can be experienced as a moment of grace.

Mary is in need of a specialist who can hear her story and guide her in theological reflection. The caregiver's verbal recognition that various moral stances are held by churches and individuals can provide Mary with a broader perspective. Many lesbians have internalized the messages of condemnation in ways that are destructive to their lives and their partnerships and have not been told often enough that there are other moral perspectives. Assisting Mary in distancing herself from debates in the church can offer her the ability to keep from feeling personally attacked as she sorts out her own feelings and perspectives.

Finding concrete ways to communicate to Mary that God affirms her sexuality and her partnership can be liberating. In the church that Mary describes, sexuality was probably not presented as something to be celebrated. Looking at the scriptures can be helpful for Mary as she discovers new images of a God who blesses the creation of sexuality. Reflecting with Mary about what it means to be a lesbian who is created as a sexual being can connect her with a spirituality that may be dormant or in need of revitalization.

The pastoral care specialist in this case may become a link between Mary, a community of faith that does not accept her, and other churches that might receive her fully. It may be that Mary eventually will need to find a worshiping community other than the one in which she was raised. Caregivers who know the pastors of accepting and affirming churches in their communities will be of great assistance to women in lesbian relationships. The pastoral caregiver can serve as a transitional figure for Mary as she explores communities of faith that might welcome her.

Mary needs a pastoral caregiver who confronts heterosexism by affirming her relationship and challenging it to grow in faithful ways. Offering a sacred space for Mary and her partner can encourage them to reflect on the qualities they would like to have at the core of their relationship. Presenting the images of covenant with its qualities of love, justice, and mutuality can provide Mary and her partner with a vision for living in faithful partnership.

Pastoral care specialists who are proactive in the community and who speak out on behalf of lesbians and gay men in their churches and denominations are persons whom lesbians and gay men will seek out for care and counseling. Working openly with lesbian partners confronts the systemic injustices that impinge upon their relationships at individual and communal levels.

Integrating Theological Reflection and Clinical Knowledge

The goal of this book is to integrate the theological reflection and clinical knowledge necessary for offering pastoral care and counseling to women in lesbian relationships. The focus is intentionally on the relationships women have with one another rather than on individual issues. While every relationship must contend with personal concerns, the aim of this book is to address the qualities necessary for lesbian covenantal partnerships. There are three interrelated purposes: to provide a pastoral theological perspective, to share basic knowledge about lesbian relationships, and to examine specific clinical concerns that emerge in pastoral counseling with women in lesbian relationships.

A Pastoral
Theological Perspective

The primary perspective presented in this book is that of a pastoral theologian and counselor whose goal is to bring the resources of theology, psychology, and experience into pastoral clinical work with women in lesbian relationships.[33] Pastoral theology is the dialogical enterprise of bringing the resources of faith to the arena of care while simultaneously allowing the experiences of listening and being with others to influence the construction of theology. It is impossible to offer pastoral care without challenging, reshaping, and reforming conceptualizations of God, faith, and community in the process.[34] Pastoral care is, primarily, a task of theological reflection. Pastoral care specialists cannot focus so exclusively on the technical and skill-oriented aspects of being therapists that they lose sight of the essential pastoral theological nature of their work.

Clarifying the basic theological assumptions that ground this work enables readers to be mindful of the foundations they bring to the tasks of pastoral care. Four assumptions, in particular, ground pastoral clinical work with women in lesbian relationships.

The first assumption is that pastoral care engages individuals and communities in theological and moral reflection. Pastoral representatives listen to the stories, the pains, and the celebrations of people not because this meets their personal needs but because they understand pastoral care to be fundamental to the church through its functions of healing, sustaining, guiding, and reconciling.[35] Individuals and families are welcomed into the sanctuary of the pastoral care office, thereby connecting care receivers and caregivers to the church's wider ministry of seeking justice and liberation, healing and wholeness.

Increasingly, pastoral care specialists are aware of the link between the prophetic voice of the church and the sanctity of the counseling office.[36] A twofold approach is required in pastoral care with women in lesbian relationships. First, pastoral care specialists must be proactive in affirming in individuals and partners their movements toward justice and wholeness. At another level, however, pastoral caregivers must participate in the church and encourage it to relate to others with the same qualities of love, justice, and mutuality. Pastoral specialists cannot be concerned only with women who choose to enter into care and counseling; they must also be diligent in their efforts to challenge ecclesial structures to support women in the nurturing of their primary relationships with one another.

A second assumption that grounds this project is that God affirms human sexuality. The works of James Nelson and Carter Heyward inform this theological perspective.[37] Both of these sexual theologians support a central claim: God affirms the embodiment of human sexuality in our relationships with one another and within the community of faith. Pastoral caregivers often work with persons caught in the complexities and vulnerabilities of attempting to discern the presence of God in their sexual relationships. Sexual theology asserts that faith perspectives, theological and ecclesial traditions, scripture, and other resources inform understandings about sexuality and its place in creation. Simultaneously, the experience of relating as sexual beings provides insight into God and God's activity in the world.

Caring with women in lesbian relationships engages pastoral theologians in affirming the goodness of sexuality in the midst of a culture and a church that often discourage women in relationship from expressing or embodying that sexuality. Pastoral theologians who are concerned not so much with the "rules" persons ought to live by but with the qualities that create covenantal partnerships are those who can affirm the God-given gift of sexuality.

A third assumption in this book is that communities of faith are places where women ought to be given the opportunity to discern what it means to live as faithful spiritual and sexual beings. The word *faithful*, as used in this context, means a steadfast and primary commitment to God, self, and others. Persons should experience congruence between their commitments of faith and their specific relationships. Communities of faith need to provide space for women to talk about, celebrate, and at times grieve the loss of their partnerships. Women in lesbian relationships wrestle with spiritual questions not because they love other women but because they are human beings endowed with the capacity to seek and yearn for communion with self, others, and God. Local congregations and churches can offer women a place for such communion.

Discernment occurs not in isolation but within the context of the broader community of faith. For lesbian partners this raises a critical issue since it is often difficult to find a church or fellowship where they can ask questions, talk about their relationships, or celebrate their covenants. The result for many women is that they feel isolated from community in their discernment processes. Pastoral representatives can be one link between lesbian partnerships and communities of faith. To be proactive means to understand that connecting women with communities where they can be affirmed is one of the primary tasks of pastoral care. Those who are in conversation and dialogue with denominational structures and churches offer lesbians some hope for a more just acceptance in the future.

A final pastoral theological assumption in this book is that women in lesbian covenantal partnerships reflect the church's normative understandings of relatedness and are to be affirmed and blessed by God and the church. Covenantal lesbian partnerships are faithful when they are built upon the normative qualities of love, justice, and mutuality. One of the gifts that pastoral care specialists offer women, their families, and their churches is the opportunity to have meaningful conversations about the qualities that promote covenantal relationships.

This book assumes that lesbian partnerships are to be affirmed. Churches, fellowships, communities of faith, and denominations that offer more than tolerance or minimal acceptance—that are genuine in their love and care for women in lesbian relationships—extend opportunities for women to experience the grace of God in community. As rituals and models for embracing the lives of lesbian partners continue to be developed, signs of liberation and justice appear in communities of faith.

Basic Knowledge for Working with Women in Lesbian Partnerships

The second purpose of this book is to provide self-education for pastoral care specialists so that they may serve the church, their parishioners, and their clients more appropriately and faithfully. To engage in pastoral care with women in lesbian partnerships and to maintain a sense of integrity requires that caregivers know something about what it means to be women who love women.

Women in lesbian relationships often voice reluctance about approaching pastoral caregivers for fear that they will be rejected, dismissed, or given sermons about their lack of moral character. Some women recall previous negative experiences with churches or pastoral representatives with whom they have shared openly. Added to this is the burden that many women feel about having to educate the pastoral caregiver about the realities of living as lesbians in relationship. While a certain amount of learning always occurs naturally in care and counseling, it is unethical to expect vulnerable care recipients to teach specialists basic information they should know. The responsibility for learning rests with pastoral care specialists, not with parishioners or clients.

Lesbians are women for whom there is an attraction to and desire to be with other women emotionally, spiritually, physically, and sexually. We are as diverse as the culture in which we live: working poor and professionally employed, educated and illiterate, persons of color and Caucasians, women with children and without, partnered and single, young and old, liberal feminists and conservative traditionalists. At the same time there are common concerns that draw the community of lesbian women together. As with many other populations with which pastoral caregivers work, these common issues emerge in diverse ways.

Specific Pastoral Clinical Dimensions

A third purpose of this book is to focus on specific pastoral clinical concerns present in caring for women in lesbian relationships. The predominant theory used in this book shows both a healthy respect for individual psychodynamic theory and for systems theory. The dynamics of particular partnerships reflect not only themes from families of origin but also the experience of living in many systems that are not open and affirming for lesbians most of the time. Fundamental to my clinical understanding is a commitment to a feminist method that challenges traditional ways of thinking about women. Offering constructive responses to concerns lesbians bring into the therapeutic experience requires that attention be given to the impact of culture and the systemic injustice of sexism and heterosexism on women and their partnerships. Individual and partnership issues are always connected to the communities in which women live.

This book is organized around themes that emerge in clinical work with women in lesbian relationships. Each chapter begins with case material and includes conversation about theological and clinical matters. Chapter 2 provides a theological and theoretical framework for thinking about the meaning of lesbian identity formation. Chapter 3 considers the nature of covenantal lesbian partnerships established around the norms of love, justice, and mutuality.

Chapter 4 examines particular challenges faced in lesbian partnerships, while chapter 5 turns to a discussion of family and the coming out process. The book concludes with a pastoral theological perspective on what it means to be engaged in proactive pastoral counseling with women in lesbian relationships and with communities of faith.

Chapter Two

Claiming a Lesbian Identity
in the Context
of Relationships

Emilia and Grace have contacted a pastoral counselor because of tensions they are experiencing in their relationship. They have known each other for fourteen months and are thinking about moving into the same house and they are both very anxious. In the initial interview they provide information about their backgrounds.

Emilia is thirty-eight and shares that she was "born a lesbian." She has participated exclusively in relationships with women since giving herself permission to be sexually active in high school. There was one brief period when a few of her friends convinced her that she should date a man just to make sure she was lesbian. That exploration lasted only a couple of months during which time Emilia felt no emotional or physical attraction to men. Emilia went to church as a child but no longer attends. She quit going to church because she got tired of hearing people negatively judge lesbians and gay men. Her parents and friends all know she is lesbian and most of them have been supportive.

Grace is forty-five and is experiencing her first relationship with another woman. Divorced from her husband after fourteen years of marriage, she has spent the past several years raising her three children, who are now young adults. Being attracted to another woman has completely surprised Grace. As she tells the story of her life, she reveals that she is struggling with whether she really is a lesbian or not. There is no doubt in Grace's mind that she is strongly committed to her relationship with Emilia, but it is difficult for Grace to think of herself as a "lesbian."

Grace reveals that recently she has found herself wondering about several things: What does God think about her loving another woman? Has God created her this way or is she making a choice to love another woman? What would those in her church think if they knew that she loved Emilia? Can she be a faithful Christian when others tell her that she is living a life of sin?

*As Grace raises her questions, Emilia begins to express some anxiety
about their future. Emilia is convinced that Grace is lesbian and finds herself being frustrated with the fact that Grace denies that part of her identity.*

The conflicts that bring Grace and Emilia into the pastoral counselor's
office pertain to their identities as lesbians. Emilia's assertion that she was
"born a lesbian" suggests that she understands this to be a natural part of
creation. Grace's questions, however, indicate that she is not sure how persons come to be lesbian or what it means to self-identify as lesbian. The development of an intimate relationship with another woman is quite often
the occasion for first reflecting about the meaning of orientation identity.
Relationships can be strained by the process of lesbian identity formation as
women move at different paces within the partnership. It is inappropriate
to question too quickly a woman's orientation just because she expresses an
internal apprehension about self-identifying as lesbian. In a world of intense
controversy over sexuality it would be unusual to find women not experiencing some level of uneasiness about being identified as lesbian. Pastoral
care specialists offer theological, as well as psychodynamic and sociocultural, perspectives to women who are exploring lesbian identities.

The purpose of this chapter is to explore the formation of lesbian identity along with its theological and psychodynamic components. Before addressing the dynamics of lesbian identity formation, several words need to
be defined.

Identity is a concept most commonly used to refer to what is essential
about someone or something. Identities are fashioned by vocational choices
(to be a farmer or doctor), by roles held within families (to be mother or
daughter), or by descriptive words referring to particular aspects of someone's life (to be a woman). An individual's comprehensive identity is the integration of the various aspects that make that person who she is.

To say that someone has a *lesbian* identity conveys various meanings.
Having a lesbian identity can mean that a woman is attracted physically and
sexually to other women. There are those who suggest that only women
who self-identify as lesbian can be called lesbian because the word indicates
an internal self-understanding that may or may not be connected to behavior. The word *lesbian* can be used to talk about the emotional closeness
women experience with other women. Others claim that being lesbian is a
political statement more than anything else. From this latter perspective,
lesbian identities point to the bonding of women with one another over
against men.[1] In this book, to self-identify as lesbian means for women to
consciously articulate that their primary affectional, sexual, and emotional
relationships are with other women. Not all women who are involved in
intimate emotional or physical relationships with other women express

their self-identity as being lesbian. The phrase "women in lesbian relationships" is used to acknowledge this reality. What makes something a "lesbian relationship" is the physical, sexual, emotional, and spiritual attachment a woman experiences with at least one other woman. The word *lesbian*, or the term *lesbian identity*, is reserved for those who self-identify in that manner.

Three other terms are important in discussions on the formation of lesbian identities: *sex, gender,* and *orientation.* While the definition of these words may be self-evident, it is helpful to briefly outline their particular contributions to lesbian identity.[2]

The word *sex* often is used in two ways. First, sex is a noun that refers to whether persons are biological males or females. Theologically this connotes meanings about being created in the image of God and being blessed with a biological component. A second popular usage of sex, although not a helpful one for lesbians, is as a reference to the physical act of intercourse. Used this way, the word focuses almost exclusively on the sexual behavior of persons rather than on the quality of their relationships.

The word *sexuality*, a broader term that refers to the human yearning and capacity to relate to persons not only physically but emotionally and spiritually, is used in this book. An assumption sometimes made is that self-identification as lesbian refers only to women's sexual and physical behaviors with other women. However, physical expression is only one aspect of what it means to be lesbian. Having a lesbian identity points toward fundamental perspectives and dispositions women bring to their primary relationships as well as to their general worldview. Self-identification as lesbian affects how women relate to others and how they are, in turn, treated by others. Lesbian identity cannot be limited to the physical sexual activity of women.

The word *sex*, when used as a description of whether persons are male or female, is often confused with *gender.* This latter term, gender, refers to the psychodynamic and social construction of men and women in the culture. What it *means* to be women in the culture stems from social, cultural, ethnic, and familial understandings that are expressed and internalized. Theological and religious resources contribute to the creation of gender by explicating such things as what it means to be a "Christian woman." Individuals may experience conflict when their internal self-understandings contradict what the culture or their families expect of them as women. For example, the socialization process encourages women to adopt gender identities as "wives" or "mothers." For many women, lesbian and straight, these expectations and internalizations create difficulties. To achieve integrated identity a person needs to balance those external expectations and internal desires.[3]

Lesbians, like all women, bring their internalizations of gender into their relationships with one another. Some women are acutely aware of the negative impact gender socialization has had on their lives. Feminists and many lesbians confront and challenge such gender constructions. Radical lesbian feminists, for example, may become separatists who seek structures outside the patriarchal culture for living and working. They are sometimes referred to as women-identified women.[4] Other women appear to be less conscious of the impact of the social and psychodynamic constructions of gender on their lives. Pastoral caregivers who offer opportunities to reflect with women in lesbian relationships about their internalizations of gender can raise their consciousness in ways that can be liberating.

Orientation signifies the primary affectional, physical, emotional, spiritual, and sexual attractions persons have for others. Primarily relating to persons of the opposite sex means a person is heterosexual in orientation. Women for whom primary affectional and sexual relationships are established with persons of the same sex are lesbian. Those who either lack clarity about their attractions or have an expressed desire to relate to both sexes are bisexual. Those who, for various reasons, do not relate at intimate sexual or emotional levels to anyone are asexual. Asexuality should not be confused with a conscious choice of celibacy at particular times in life.

None of these orientations should be interpreted as being fixed or static entities. Instead they are meant to reflect self-understandings persons have at particular times in their lives. For example, women who eventually come to understand themselves as lesbian may previously have been in heterosexual marriages or in other relationships where their self-identities were heterosexual. For a variety of reasons, self-definition can shift over time. This should not be interpreted as indicating neurotic or unhealthy personalities.

In this book the term *orientation identity* is used rather than *sexual preference*. The word *preferences* indicates that persons have choices over their intimate relationships and sexual identity. It does not imply, however, that people capriciously choose their orientation or their relationships. Those scholars who use the term *sexual preferences* want to avoid any connotation that being lesbian is something that is dependent upon a fixed or biologically driven reality. While some women do understand themselves as having been born as lesbians, many others come to their lesbian identities through circuitous routes and after experiencing many divergent choices.[5]

While this notion of preference is supported in this book, the word *orientation* is used to illuminate another aspect of lesbian identity. Women who love women bring a different worldview to the creation of meaningful relationships. They are "oriented," or positioned, in their families, their churches, and the culture in a manner that gives them a unique vantage point. This does not mean that every lesbian understands and interprets the world only through the lenses of her sexual experiences and relationships. Instead, the word *orientation* suggests that women in lesbian relationships cannot escape the fact that their stance toward the world around them is affected by their primary affectional, emotional, spiritual, and sexual partnerships.

The term *orientation identity* is used to note that most women who love women develop, over time, an internal self-identity as lesbians. Short-term relationships that may not be lasting still have an impact on the lives of the women involved in significant ways. While some may never come to self-identify as lesbians, all women who love women must move through a process of deciding what it means to be involved in a lesbian relationship. There are women who claim that their lesbian identities provide the primary lens through which they experience all life. The term *lesbian* may have less to do with sexual behavior in relationships and more to do with the internal perceptions women bring to those relationships.[6]

Identity never develops in a vacuum; it always develops in the context of broader cultural and social realities. For example, lesbian women of color deal with what Beverly Greene calls "triple jeopardy." Not only must they face the biases of being women and loving other women, but they have the added factors of their ethnicity. The way that race and orientation integrate into the identities of lesbians of color remains a matter for ongoing research.[7]

Many philosophical, theological, and political concerns rest underneath these brief definitions of terms, and it is beyond the scope of this chapter to address those concerns. The remainder of this chapter focuses on three aspects of identity: theological reflections on identity, psychodynamic theory and the social construction of lesbian identity, and perspectives on the developmental process of lesbian identity formation.

Theological Resources for Identity

One responsibility for pastoral caregivers is reflecting upon the theological meaning of identity. This is especially true when working with lesbians on issues of identity formation. Too often theological reflections are dismissed in favor of seemingly more pertinent psychodynamic theories. Four activities in pastoral care provide specialists with theological visions about lesbian identity formation: naming and being named, embracing sexuality, connecting spirituality, and moving toward liberation. These four activities are theological in their content, thereby contributing to a distinctively pastoral clinical approach for working with lesbian women.

First, the theological action of *naming* is pertinent for women like Grace and Emilia. Grace is not only asking questions about her identity but reflecting upon what it means to be *named* as a lesbian or to *claim that name* for herself. Women usually move from rather timid considerations of the possibility of being lesbian toward more public declarations of their identities. In the process they both claim a name for themselves as lesbian and are named by others.

Naming is an important theological component of identity throughout much of Hebrew and Christian traditions. The importance given to the process of naming in creation, the claiming of particular names throughout the scriptures, the changes in names signifying important assertions about identity, the attention given to naming lineage, the naming of Jesus, and the tradition's promise that God calls people by name all witness to the powerful meanings attached to naming.[8]

While naming may seem to be a rather elementary issue, it is critical in working with women in lesbian relationships. Listening to the names they use to identify themselves provides insight into the meanings they attach to their relationships. For example, to acknowledge that one is involved in a lesbian relationship can carry the consequence of marginalization in church communities.

The power of *being named* by others as lesbian also carries significance. To know someone's name, or that person's story, grants one person power over another. Someone who knows another's name can choose whom to tell, when to tell, or whether to tell others about that name.[9] Many risks are involved in being named as lesbian. Negative reactions from others can eventuate in loss of job security, changes in relationships with family and friends, or the denial of status in the church.

At the same time, *claiming the name* of lesbian can cultivate internal strengths present in women. For example, when women draw upon their name as lesbians, they have clarity about who they understand themselves to be and about a primary community of support upon which they can rely in the face of adversity or potential losses. Theologically, naming and being named can bring not only potential losses but experiences of grace.

The second action, *embracing sexuality*, means recognizing that God has given the gift of being sexual to humans. Sexuality is, in part, the vehicle through which persons experience longing and attachment, communion and community. James Nelson and Sandra Longfellow note in their introduction to *Sexuality and the Sacred:*

> Theologically, we believe that human sexuality, while including God's gift of the procreative capacity, is most fundamentally the divine invitation to find our destinies not in loneliness but in deep connection. To the degree that it is free from the distortions of unjust and abusive power relations, we experience our sexuality as the basic eros of our humanness that urges, invites, and lures us out of our loneliness into intimate communication and communion with God and the world. . . . Sexuality, in sum, is the physiological and emotional grounding of our capacities to love.[10]

The concept of eros has become important in sexual theology, particularly in the works of Carter Heyward and in the writings of lesbian African American poet Audre Lorde.[11] For Heyward, the depth of the incarnation of a loving and caring God can be witnessed in genuine and deep relatedness with others. She states:

> The erotic is our most fully embodied experience of the love of God. As such, it is the source of our capacity for transcendence, the "crossing over" among ourselves, making connections between ourselves in relation. The erotic is the divine Spirit's yearning, through our bodyselves, toward mutually empowering relation, which is our most fully embodied experience of God as love.[12]

God is incarnate as persons express their sexuality and experience it with others.

Many women, either in the silence of their souls or in the context of pastoral conversations, wonder about whether God loves their expressions of sexuality, and by implication, whether God loves them. The voicing of these concerns should not be interpreted as a sign that someone is uncomfortable with her sexuality. Rather, the ambivalence that is expressed often reflects the depth of theological questions that emerge in the context of being sexual. Embracing sexuality means facing theological questions with integrity.

For the pastoral theologian, women in lesbian relationships offer resources for reflecting theologically upon issues of power in relationships, of sexuality that is not defined by traditional understandings of sex, of mutuality within a committed but not legally defined relationship, and of movements toward justice within the context of broader communities. These realities ultimately offer insight into the nature of God. To deny or to minimize lesbian experience as being outside the realm of God's creation does an injustice to the ongoing revelation of God's being. To embrace sexuality means opening the community of faith to new understandings and insights about God gained by theological reflection with women in lesbian relationships.[13]

A third activity, *connecting spirituality*, is closely related to the concept of eros described above. Connecting spirituality is a theological task as those places of passion in the lives of women are affirmed and blessed. Spirituality is not divorced from sexuality; rather, it is intimately connected to experiences of communion and intimacy. Through spirituality persons are connected to Something that transcends and yet remains immanent.

In contemporary culture there is confusion about the meaning of spirituality. The word *spirituality* best signifies the connection of individuals to humanity and ultimately to God. Toinette Eugene offers this definition:

Spirituality is no longer identified simply with asceticism, mysticism, the practice of virtue, and methods of prayer. Spirituality, i.e., the human capacity to be self-transcending, relational, and freely committed, encompasses all of life, including our human sexuality.[14]

The intersection between sexuality and spirituality comes alive as persons live in relationship to one another. As women in lesbian relationships experience the sensuality of their intimacy, they encounter places of deep passion and love, which often offer them a sense of God's presence or love. The intensity of feeling loved sensually, completely, and unconditionally connects spirituality with sexuality. Chris Glaser, a gay man denied ordination in the Presbyterian Church, notes that

[s]exuality and spirituality are not opposing forces, as is frequently supposed today. Instead, both draw people into relationship. Sexuality draws us into physical relationships: hugging, holding, caressing, and most intimately as lovers, kissing and intercourse. Spirituality draws us into relationships that both include and transcend bodies because it includes and transcends that which is visible.[15]

Pastoral caregivers can provide written resources to help women connect with their spirituality as lesbians. For example, Craig O'Neill and Kathleen Ritter suggest that spirituality can guide persons toward the affirmation of goodness, a sense of community, and the Creator.[16] They note that while "some gay or lesbian people feel a profound alienation with regard to organized religion, others who have never bonded with a faith tradition experience an inner void that can only be called spiritual."[17] What O'Neill and Ritter correctly assert is that women seeking pastoral care often are looking for spiritual grounding and transformation.

Pastoral caregivers who are authentic in their desire to care for the souls as well as for the minds, psyches, and relationships of lesbians should encourage conversations about spirituality. Tapping into the passionate lives that women have with one another engages them in rediscovering the passion of a God who cares deeply about their souls. Connecting spirituality to the passion of loving relationships brings renewed energy to weary hearts and souls.

The fourth activity, *moving toward liberation*, recognizes that claiming a lesbian identity can be extremely painful, yet freeing. Liberation is the process of moving out of bondage from systems that oppress, if not actively persecute, lesbians. Pastoral caregivers should affirm that God seeks liberation for all persons.

Many women experience daily oppression, resulting in feelings of anger or despair. The pressure to maintain a secret way of life may take so much emotional energy that women are not free to thrive in their relationships, their vocations, or their lives. Women may experience the oppression of families who seek to destroy their relationships with other women or who strive to convert them to heterosexual orientations. Other oppressive structures include: the attempt to restrict civil rights of lesbians in several states, the lack of access to privileges granted to legally married couples, the exclusion from particular vocations because of lesbian orientation, the fear of losing children during custody battles, and the pressure to participate in traditional heterosexual relationships.[18]

Caregivers who connect women with supportive systems that are specifically designed to meet the needs of lesbians offer them an opportunity to move toward liberation with others. Pastoral caregivers should be familiar with the places of worship that support lesbians, the groups that are defined by their care for lesbians, and the places where lesbians in the community connect with one another. Renewal and fortification occur as lesbians discover they are not alone.

Another way that women may experience liberating pastoral care is with specialists who are knowledgeable about the stories of lesbian and gay persons in the culture and in history. Knowing that the movement toward liberation has spanned many years can be freeing for women as they connect their stories with those of others who have gone before. Dan Spencer, writing about ministry with lesbian and gay persons, states:

> [S]elf-identification is critical to liberation of subjugated groups and peoples. This process includes claiming personal and communal history, as well as reclaiming the group's history from the distortions and mystification of the dominant perspective.[19]

Spencer's assertion implies that self-identifying as lesbians connects women to a broader historical reality, and they experience the transformation that comes in hearing the stories of other lesbians and gay men.[20]

Finally, women in lesbian relationships sometimes seek opportunities to participate in liberating activities, not only for themselves but for others. Some women become advocates in the political or legal arena, in the AIDS crisis, or in other issues important to women. Many lesbians make intentional choices about how they live in the world, who will share their lives, and what it means to be participants in a more just and liberating world. As noted above, claiming a name activates internal and external power. Pastoral caregivers who are sensitive to the movements of liberation can assist women in lesbian relationships to think not just about their individual lives and relationships but also about creating justice in the world.

Women who have commitments of faith or who are connected to churches and communities often seek ways to participate in liberating activities within the context of church. At times this means challenging churches on their moral stances toward homosexuality. Many women join social concern organizations supported by their denominations or local churches. Communities of faith that welcome and affirm lesbian relationships are already at work in movements toward liberation. Assuming that being lesbian is congruent with faithful living invites women to enter broader struggles for justice as they recognize that liberation movements are connected.

Pastoral caregivers have unique opportunities to deal theologically with what it means for women to identify as lesbians or to have lesbian relationships. Pastoral care specialists are called upon to offer sacred spaces to women as they name themselves as lesbians, embrace their sexuality, connect their spirituality with the passion of their lives, and move toward liberation.

Theoretical Perspectives
on Lesbian Identity

Pastoral care specialists who work with women like Grace and Emilia need theoretical perspectives for approaching lesbian identity formation. Care specialists have an obligation to respond to questions asked of them by parishioners, clients, families, and churches, such as: Are women born as lesbians? What does the scientific community say about the causes of lesbian identity? Are lesbian identities the result of inadequate parenting? Can women change from heterosexual to lesbian orientation? While there are few clear answers, caregivers can become conversant with various theories in an attempt to respond genuinely to concerns people raise.

In examining insights from psychodynamic theory, biological determinism, and the social construction of identity, pastoral caregivers need to remember that women who self-identify as lesbians do not need justifications for who they are. An exploration into theoretical perspectives illustrates that none of them are conclusive or definitive statements about the etiology of lesbian orientations. Theories that are used to dismiss, destroy, or pathologize women in lesbian relationships are damaging to women and their families. However, pastoral caregivers who are familiar with different theoretical vantage points should come away with an increased appreciation for the complexity of lesbian identity.

Etiology and
Psychodynamic Theory

Much of the psychodynamic literature on homosexuality leans heavily upon the medical model of illness and cure. As a result, it is not surprising that, prior to the 1970s in particular, strands of theoretical literature were concerned with uncovering the causes of homosexuality and, in turn,

searching for potential "cures" for persons with this "disorder."[21] The desire to discover the etiology of lesbianism is not as strong as it once was.
However, in the general culture and in religious communities considerable
discussion still arises about what "makes" women become lesbian.

Pastoral caregivers would do well to attend to the literature on the etiology of homosexuality for two reasons. First, those who desire to be proactive in ministering with individuals, partnerships, families, and churches
need to challenge popular and traditional notions that are inadequate for or
derogatory to lesbians. Second, psychology continues to be a major resource for pastoral care and counseling. Hoping the social sciences are more
precise than theology, many pastoral care specialists have come to rely upon
psychodynamic theories to explain homosexuality. Kristine Falco notes in
Psychotherapy with Lesbian Clients that the growing faith in social sciences has
resulted in significant shifts of perspectives.

> [I]n the last few centuries of Western culture in particular, lesbianism has
> moved from being considered a theological-moral phenomenon (a sin),
> to being considered a legal matter (a crime), to most recently being con-
> sidered a medical-psychological phenomenon (a mental illness).[22]

Women, their families, and churches often express a desire to understand what causes homosexuality. The psychological community does not
agree on the etiology of homosexuality, even though most traditional psychoanalysts have maintained a rather conservative interpretation. This
heritage can be traced, in large part, to traditional Freudian attitudes and
theories about sexuality.[23]

While Sigmund Freud's interpretation of homosexuality continues to
be the foundation for various understandings of lesbianism as pathology,
two things must be considered about Freud. First of all, Freud was primarily interested in male homosexuality and paid little attention to women
who were attracted to women. His theory is male-oriented and patriarchal
in its structure. While this, in and of itself, does not completely discredit
his perspective, it does suggest particular limitations when applying it as a
theoretical grounding for understanding lesbian orientation identity.

Second, many argue that Freud was ambivalent about the moral dilem-
mas surrounding homosexuality. Freud did not rebuke homosexual persons; he understood homosexuality to be a result of abnormal development. Kenneth Lewes, in an insightful book examining Freudian theory,
points out that Freud cannot be interpreted as a strict moralist who argues
that all lesbian or gay male behavior is inherently to be condemned. For
example, in a letter to an American mother of a gay man, Freud does not
judge her son but suggests that he is experiencing a "variation of the sexual function produced by a certain arrest of sexual development."[24] What
is clear in Freud is a commitment to heterosexuality as sexually normative.

He believed that bisexuality, while apparent in early childhood, has its most productive and natural outcome in heterosexual relationships.[25]

Four psychodynamic constructs, all of which originate in Freudian theory, appear in the literature on the etiology of homosexuality.[26] The first of these theoretical constructs suggests that developmental arrests, particularly in the form of fixations on the mothering figure in childhood, eventuate in obstructing adults from reaching heterosexual maturity. Freud outlines a linear developmental process where persons move from one stage to another in a sequential manner. The goal is for persons to be able to engage in positive heterosexual relationships. Developmental arrests prevent persons from such relationships.

A second theoretical construct claims that male homosexuals exhibit castration fear, in which a male "fears that sexual intercourse [with a woman] may castrate him."[27] In this view, men who love men are afraid that sexual intercourse with women will take away their male powers. Perhaps the complementary theory for lesbianism is voiced in the hypothesis that women are afraid of having their power usurped by men and are, therefore, involved with other women. Rather than castration fear, the power of "penis envy" is present in this theory, suggesting that women attracted to other women pretend to have a power that they do not have as women.

Narcissism is a third theoretical construct present in the psychodynamic literature. This theory claims that persons fall in love with their own beings and therefore develop intimate sexual relationships with persons who are like them. This interpretation suggests that women who are in relationships with other women are actually in love with the image of themselves and are incapable or unwilling to love men, who represent their opposite.

Finally, a fourth theoretical construct claims that homosexuality occurs when a "person has identified too much with a member of the opposite sex, usually the parent, and has copied an erotic bent which [s]he should not have copied."[28] In this perspective etiology is traced to inappropriate opposite sexual identifications during the completion of the Oedipal phase. For women this means that they have over-identified with their fathers, thereby making it difficult to separate from them or to fall in love with other men.

Contemporary theories that interpret homosexuality negatively build upon these constructs in various ways. Lesbian identities are understood by some as "a symptom of a severe personality disorder" in which contributing factors might include such things as inadequate parenting, psychic trauma from rape or incest, influences from peers and/or the environment, or seduction by other homosexual people.[29] In conversations with parishioners and clients, pastoral care specialists should watch for belief systems that inform the understandings of lesbian identity. When appropriate, theoretical perspectives that pathologize or destructively interpret lesbian identity should be challenged.

All theories should be used judiciously and carefully. Many illustrations show how they can harm women in lesbian relationships or their families. For example, many fathers and mothers feel overly responsible for their daughters' sexual identities, resulting in excessive guilt and shame. While some theories might suggest that parents have some responsibility for the sexual identities of their daughters, these are only tentative conclusions of one perspective and should not be interpreted as holding the truth about women who love women.

Notions that convey the belief that all women in lesbian relationships are afraid of men or hate men should also be challenged. Some women morally prefer not to structure their lives around heterosexual and patriarchal norms. To use theoretical constructs about abnormal development to negatively judge lesbians is unethical. Similarly, to use a theoretical construct that associates lesbian identity with a fear of men is to deny that many lesbians have strong male friendships.[30]

Every theory has its strengths and weaknesses and can be used in helpful or destructive ways. Proactive pastoral caregivers need to pay particular attention to interpretations of lesbian identities as a form of pathology or illness. Understandings of pathology are as dependent upon the culture as they are upon particular theories or sets of clinical observations. For example, Lewes suggests that there is much about Freudian theory that remains bound to its particular place in history.[31] This does not mean that the theory should be dismissed; rather, it challenges scholars to continue to clarify the contributions of various theories in light of contemporary research.

One example of the effect of ongoing research on changing theoretical perspectives is offered by Alfred Kinsey's work. In the mid-1950s Kinsey's research on sexual behaviors advanced understandings that were an alternative to those proposed by the psychoanalytic field. After extensive interviews, the research team discovered that only a small percentage of people reported exclusively heterosexual or exclusively homosexual behaviors. For example, the research found "that 37 percent of the male population had some homosexual experience to the point of orgasm between adolescence and old age, 13 percent had more homosexual than heterosexual experience, and 4 percent were exclusively homosexual."[32] Thus, approximately half the men interviewed had engaged in sexual behaviors with same-sex partners. Women reported similar experiences in their sexual behavior.

Kinsey and his colleagues developed what has come to be known as the Kinsey scale. This seven-point scale attempts to place women and men on a continuum between exclusively homosexual and exclusively heterosexual behaviors. As with all theories, Kinsey's conclusions have their limitations. It should be remembered, for example, that what Kinsey measured was sexual behavior, not internal orientation identity. As noted in the definitions given early in this chapter, while the two are related, they are not synonymous. In a similar vein, Kinsey's scale appears to show a dualistic continuum that has been challenged by contemporary scholars. Nonetheless, Kinsey's research contributed to a greater openness on the part of theoreticians by demonstrating that same-sex behavior was much more common than had been previously thought.[33]

About the time Kinsey's research appeared, Evelyn Hooker presented a paper to the 1956 annual meeting of the American Psychological Association titled "The Adjustment of the Male Overt Homosexual." The core of her research determined that there were no major differences in adjustment between men who identified as heterosexual and those who were gay.[34] The work of Kinsey, Hooker, and others began to "normalize" the experience of lesbians and gay men within the culture. As a result, questions about the cause of homosexuality slowly began to give way to concerns for the health and well-being of lesbians and gay men. Therapists began to talk directly about issues that lesbians and gay men brought to counseling rather than about how to change orientations.

A significant step was taken in 1973, when homosexuality was withdrawn from the list of psychological disorders designated by the American Psychiatric Association and the American Psychological Association.[35] This change did not come without conflict and disagreement. While homosexuality is no longer considered a pathology, a category "ego dystonic homosexuality" has been added to the Diagnostic and Statistical Manual and can be diagnosed in instances where

> one desires to be a heterosexual and rejects intensely her or his homosexuality. But this does not take into account the sociological facts that could induce such self-hatred, and suggests once again that homosexuality rather than social prejudice is the problem which needs to be "cured."[36]

The diagnosis of "ego-dystonic" should be used cautiously and should be limited to persons who are so uncomfortable with their sexuality that they are unable to function.

It is common for women to express discomfort with their emerging sexual identity as lesbians in a culture that actively discourages them from living openly as lesbians. This internal discomfort should not be equated with latent heterosexuality or with pathology. Perhaps those from the Boston Lesbian Psychologies Collective have said it best:

> Implicit in the psychodynamic models that underlie much current thinking is the notion that discomfort means something is amiss—something that must be overcome by the lesbian individual, couple, or community. In contrast, views that take account of both the external forces impinging on lesbians and the impact of those forces on internal responses might interpret discomfort as a critical indication of awareness and coping. Thus,

discomfort would become an indicator of creative adjustment rather than pathology.[37]

Women who experience discomfort in their self-identification as lesbian are reflecting the difficulty and pain of living in a culture where their choices to love women are very rarely affirmed.

Biology and Orientation

The connections between biology, genetics, and sexual orientation are pursued by scientists in various ways. One example of this research can be found in the work of John Money. By examining sex hormones and their influence upon the prenatal brain Money argues that "the prenatal hormonolization of the brain influences the subsequent sexual status or orientation as bisexual, heterosexual, or homosexual."[38] Through elaborate discussions about the prenatal origins of homosexuality, differences in brain structures, and several other methods of research, Money attempts to clarify the connection between biology and orientation.

What is unknown about the inner workings of humans is considerable. While it is naive to assume that no connection exists between biology and orientation, the way in which biological contributions are to be understood in reflections on homosexuality is unclear. The possibility that persons are created at birth as homosexuals encourages many persons to affirm lesbians and gays. Others believe that persons born as homosexuals are like persons who carry a birth defect with them throughout their lives. Still others are convinced that God does not create homosexuality. Whether or not researchers discover a genetic or biological link to homosexual orientation, individuals and communities must still discern what such a link or the lack thereof actually means in the moral debates about homosexuality.

Like the psychodynamic research outlined above, the theories involving biology and orientation must be placed within a broader framework. Pastoral caregivers may not be able to assess the validity of the research unless they have special training in this area. However, they can attend to how these theoretical perspectives are used either to liberate persons or to oppress them. From this perspective there are several factors to consider.

First, the research linking biology or genetics to homosexuality may be an area where the concerns of lesbians and gay men are different. Much of the research focuses on men, while women seem less concerned with proving that homosexuality is attributable to biological factors. Questions of biology and genetics lead many women to raise concerns about essentialist claims. Essentialism, in part, is the theoretical assertion that there are primary qualities that make persons who they are. Often what is understood to be essential are biological realities, such as skin color or identification as males and females. Essentialism argues, for example, that women are fundamentally different from men because of the distinctiveness of their biology. Often notions of essentialism lead to assumptions that all women or all men share particular characteristics or qualities, often not taking into account social and environmental factors. Thus, there is a growing suspicion of "essentialism" within feminist literature.[39]

In a similar way, essentialism suggests that there are ontological differences between being lesbian and being heterosexual. These qualities are understood to be determined by biology and are static and fixed rather than fluid and dynamic. Arguing against this perspective, researchers John De Cecco and John Elia suggest that

> [b]iological essentialism depicts a process in which the biological influences precede the cultural influences and set pre-determined biological limits to the effects culture can have in shaping sexual and gender expression. It assumes that each biological ingredient (i.e., genes, hormones, and brain tissue) is an independent agent that, in some additive and sequential fashion, exerts its influence without itself undergoing change. Since the ingredients are conceived as fixed entities, they result in fixed products.[40]

The difficulty with essentialism as a basis for lesbianism is that it destroys, or at least distorts, the fundamental ways in which persons are different regardless of their biological similarities. For example, not all lesbians or all heterosexual persons experience their sexuality in precisely the same manner. That women share genetic dispositions does not mean the qualities that emerge in their lives are identical. Many other factors impinge upon individuals in the process of developing identity.

In this light, Jay Paul responds to what he views as a resurgence of the biological models of sexuality:

> [T]he research to date suffers from (1) a failure to differentiate such concepts as gender identity, gender role and sexual orientation, (2) a reliance upon potentially inappropriate dichotomies in describing such concepts, (3) problematic interpretations of research that makes few distinctions between human sexual behavior and sexual behavior among rodents, and (4) the contradictions implicit in seeking simple biological determinants of constructs (such as cross-gender behavior) that are culturally determined.[41]

Sexuality is a complex aspect of being human. While there may be genetic and biological components to self-identities, ultimately as women make choices about lesbian relationships they are influenced by many factors, including their education, socioeconomic class, families of origin, friendship systems, past relationships, and internal beliefs. Approaches to understanding sexuality should not be as simplistic or reductionistic as some biological models might suggest.

To question biological essentialism is not an attempt to minimize the very real comfort that some lesbians and their families feel when they believe that women can be created biologically as lesbians. It is conceivable, and even reassuring, to grant that God's richness in creation is not limited to heterosexuality. However, asserting that it is possible for God to create women as lesbians does not imply that persons are born only lesbian or heterosexual and that, therefore, they make no choices about their orientation or behavior. Creation also involves the ongoing process of women coming to know themselves in the midst of relationships, in sometimes surprising ways.

The Social Construction of Homosexuality

A helpful supplement to the other theories and views cited in this chapter is the framework offered by the notion of the social construction of knowledge and experience. All identities are shaped and formed in social contexts. Hence, how women understand their identities is directly related to the meanings that are carried in the broader culture. For example, women not only bring the meanings they attach to their self-identification as lesbians but also incorporate the messages that have come to them from religion, public sentiment, or other institutions. A social construction perspective places the agency for integrating and solidifying an identity with individual persons in the context of social realities. Women construct their identities from "the social meaning attached to sexual and affectional preferences."[42]

Thomas Weinberg, writing about the social construction of gay men, notes the different social definitions implicit in self-identification. He states that "[d]eveloping an identity is a complex process that includes the ability to symbolize, to think abstractly, to interpret events and attitudes, to impute motives, and so on, in interaction with others."[43] Thus, as women participate in relationships, they also move through a process of thinking about what it means for them to be in relationship. Being in a lesbian relationship symbolizes something different from being in a heterosexual marriage. Trying to understand the complexity of what lesbian relationships mean to individuals, families, churches, and the culture is a task for those scholars who work out of the perspective of social construction theory.

The work of political lesbians and radical feminist separatists is most helpful and intriguing from this perspective. While few pastoral caregivers will ever be called upon to counsel radical women about their relationships, the literature they produce can be helpful in working with women in lesbian relationships. Much of the writing that arises from within the more politically radical field of lesbians reflects deep disagreement with psychotherapy as a model for empowering women in lesbian relationships. Celia Kitzinger and Rachel Perkins, for example, suggest that the whole notion of counseling is contradictory to any notions of healing within the lesbian feminist movement. In therapy persons give their power over to those who are the counselors. What is needed, according to Kitzinger and Perkins, is a valuing of the everyday expertise and care women give one another.[44]

Pastoral caregivers can value the care of women by attending to ways in which lesbian relationships are constructed, particularly taking into account the impact of religious ideation and the idealization of women evidenced in traditional marriages. Women who love women often have to come to terms not only with misconceptions about orientation but also with core images of women in this culture. Lesbians challenge the meanings about relationships that have long been promoted and maintained in the institutions of our culture. Pastoral caregivers can learn about new paradigms for constructing mutual relationships in their work with women in lesbian relationships.

Pastoral care specialists can use the vantage point of social construction theory when working with women like Grace and Emilia. Probing their perceptions, understandings, and thought processes about the meanings they attach to their relationship and orientation identities can provide insight into the dynamics of the relationship. What does it mean, for example, that Emilia understands herself as a lesbian from birth? What meaning does Grace attach to her reluctance to self-identify as lesbian even though she is in a primary emotional, affectional, and sexual relationship with another woman? A sensitive pastoral caregiver also will explore the concepts of gender that Grace and Emilia maintain in their relationship.[45] Pastoral representatives offer sacred spaces for women to reflect on their journeys as they develop their lesbian identities.

The Emergence of Lesbian Identity

Identity is both a stable and a dynamic entity. Its stability is evident as internal transformations occur slowly, although there may be times when a dramatic shift appears to result in a sudden change in someone's behavior or attitude. Usually closer examination shows that the sudden change took shape over time. Normally persons are not capricious about adopting a new internal sexual orientation or identity. Persons alter their self-perceptions through the dynamic processes of identity formation, sometimes making significant new choices about their lives. The fluid quality of identity formation means that the emergence of a lesbian self-identity marks only one aspect of identity, yet it is an aspect with tremendous power.

Some women move quickly through the process; others shift more slowly. For many women the path toward self-identification as lesbian is complicated by disclosures that bring with them significant potential losses.[46] Women may be in traditional marriages when they discover their attractions to other women, or more often to one woman in particular. In the process some women may discern that they are not lesbian or do not want to live in a lesbian relationship. Others make choices that move them toward a stronger self-identification as lesbian. Pastoral caregivers are not called to judge how persons move through the process but to engage parishioners and clients in meaningful ways as their identities evolve.

Vivienne Cass, a clinical psychologist who has researched the development of sexual orientation identity, offers a model for thinking about the formation of lesbian identity. Her paradigm is one of many that provide a framework for reflecting upon the transitions women make in claiming lesbian identities.[47] According to Cass, the process of lesbian formation is a complex one in which identity is shaped through a variety of interactive elements. Overt and covert messages from employers, colleagues, pastors, churches, and other social institutions have a profound bearing upon the emerging identity of a woman in a lesbian relationship.

Cass notes that there are subjective and objective sides of lesbian identity. The subjective refers to the internal experience women have of knowing themselves as lesbian. The objective side contains the cognitive picture women have of themselves as lesbian, including social images and understandings related to being lesbian. As Cass suggests,

> [t]he subjective side of identity . . . is the feeling or sensation a person has of *being* a homosexual. It is a *knowing* and experiencing of the self at any moment as opposed to the objective aspect of identity, which refers to *thinking about* the self. People may differ in the strength with which they feel themselves to be a homosexual/gay man/lesbian.[48]

These two aspects of development converge on the valuation given to orientation identity and how women experience and express their self-identity as lesbians. Emilia and Grace, from the opening case study, offer different perspectives on the subjective and objective side of their identities.

Women may not perceive themselves as lesbians, but friends or acquaintances may attach this name to them or to their relationships. Richard Troiden talks about this as the difference between self-identity (when persons see themselves as lesbian), perceived identity (when others view persons as lesbian), and presented identity (how persons present themselves in concrete settings).[49] There is a potential for internal conflict as women experience discrepancies between how they perceive themselves and how they are viewed by others. Pastoral caregivers can attend to the anxieties that are expressed as women seek congruence between these various aspects of identity.

Using a developmental frame, Cass outlines stages through which women move, suggesting that they be understood as linear. This paradigm is most helpful when used to assess how a person is making sense and meaning of her identity during a given period of life.[50] Rather than understanding these stages as fixed entities through which all women move in linear and orderly fashion, I would suggest they be seen as fluid and dynamic interpretations women bring to their self-understandings at different points in their journeys. Often a movement from one perspective to another is met by resistance, fear, or lack of support, making it difficult to fully embrace what Cass describes as the qualities of a given stage. Hence, the fluctuation and shifts between stages is experienced in ways that may look chaotic. Perceptive pastoral caregivers will find ways to honor women as they experience these shifting ways of self-understanding.

Women resolve their movement through each stage in different ways, since lesbian identities may be experienced as long-lasting but are not necessarily fixed and permanent.[51] Someone may find comfort in a particular phase and remain there for some time as she explores what it means to be lesbian from that perspective. Women can also feel propelled to move to the next stage as they seek greater congruence between their internal and external lives. Still other women may abandon the process, often for valid and important reasons. There are times when self-identification as lesbian is either not accurate to a person's self-understanding or is not emotionally possible. Pastoral caregivers must take into account the tremendous social pressure women experience to fit into the normative way of being in the world.

The first stage that Cass describes is *identity confusion*, as women internally wrestle with whether their feelings or actions might be considered to be lesbian.[52] Troiden suggests that prior to these initial feelings, persons are consciously aware of what it means to be lesbian. For those who recognize their orientation identity early in life, the experiences of marginality or of being different can be acute, since women are socialized early in life not to think of themselves as lesbian. Adolescents, as well as some adults, may experience strong emotions of confusion without having the words to verbalize their feelings or the concepts necessary to think about identity.[53]

Identity confusion emerges when women internally examine their sexual orientations. The reason for the questioning may be as subtle as a growing awareness of stronger emotional connections with women than with men. Or a woman might find herself involved with another woman either emotionally or sexually. A rather common scenario is for confusion to appear after a woman has been married to a man and has had children. This situation may result in an attempt to maintain a heterosexual marriage while simultaneously exploring a lesbian relationship. Generally, lesbian women arrive at their lesbian identity later in life than do gay men.[54] During this stage it is important for pastoral caregivers to respect the length of time it may take for women to make choices. Premature resolution of this stage can be injurious to women in the process of discovery.

Closure can happen in any stage. One form of closure occurs when women deny their interest in other women and reject any kind of internal lesbian feelings.[55] Women may avoid situations where they know that other lesbians are present, or they may avoid "looking" lesbian by dressing more femininely. Some women who are even more radical in their rejection of being lesbian may speak out against lesbians or join political and religious campaigns that focus on more traditional "family values."

Some women move from one stage to another by reinterpreting or reconstructing their past in light of their current experiences. A common way to express this shift in self-understanding is to claim that they have been lesbian all along and are just now beginning to realize it.[56] Others propose that their affiliations with women are just intimate friendships and not lesbian relationships. Denying they are lesbian, some women find reasons to explain why their sexual attractions were appropriate in this one instance.[57] An alternative way of transition from the first stage is for women to affirm their same-sex feelings and attractions. After weighing the risks and benefits of self-identity as lesbian women, they move into "the first step toward commitment to a homosexual self-image."[58]

In the second stage, *identity comparison*, persons move from the tentative thought that they "may" be homosexual toward the more general acknowledgement that they "probably are" lesbian. During this phase women experiment with what it might mean to self-identify as lesbian. By disclosing their identities to close friends or siblings, women explore what might be lost or gained by being lesbian. If women understand the risks to be too high, they do not continue in their lesbian identity formation. In contemplating the risks, women can also begin to realize benefits that they had not previously imagined. For example, the fear of losing custody of their children can cause women to retreat from pursuing a lesbian identity. Yet despite that fear, some women push forward, trusting that the benefits of openness and honesty will benefit their children as well as themselves.

The third stage is *identity tolerance*. At this point women move from wondering whether they might be lesbian to internally knowing that they are attracted to women and are lesbian. This is a time of partial self-acceptance. Women affirm themselves internally but may not be convinced they want to move any farther in the process. Communities of lesbian women can provide role models and mentors, encouraging women to deepen their commitments to their self-understandings. Particularly during this period, pastoral caregivers will want to be able to offer specific places women can go to meet other women and to socialize.

Identity acceptance is the fourth stage. Increased clarity about internal identity leads to more secure feelings about how others perceive and view women's lesbian identities. The difficulty of self-disclosure is apparent as women are more eager for others to know about their lesbianism, yet still have some friends they choose not to tell. During this stage women are both internally accepting and comfortable with their identities yet somewhat anxious about others knowing. There is tension as women recognize that they still fit into the straight community but are less comfortable than before with persons who do not know about their orientation identity. Pastoral care specialists can provide the affirmation necessary for women to feel good about choosing when to disclose their identities to others.

Identity pride is Cass's fifth stage. Lesbians are caught in the conflict of their positive self-affirmation and cultural rejection of their orientation. Anger often emerges in this stage as women recognize how much they give up in order to live a double life, sometimes openly as lesbians and being assumed to be straight women at other times. Leaving institutions or relationships that were once comfortable but are now experienced as not being open and affirming enough results in significant loss during this stage. Women who experience the church as an increasingly uncomfortable place to be may leave in search of more lesbian-affirming places. Others remain connected to the church but carry around the anger of not being fully accepted. Pastoral caregivers who can empathize with the pain and anger and who can become advocates for lesbians will be most helpful for women in this stage.

Lesbian pride gives way to the sixth stage, *identity synthesis.* At this point a woman maintains commitment to being lesbian while understanding that sexual orientation is but one piece of her more comprehensive identity. The anger and pride of the previous stage gives way to an understanding that women who love women are one of several minority groups who experience oppression. Women may feel less obligated during this stage to take issue with every injustice. Troiden suggests that in this stage of commitment sexuality and emotional responses come together in a whole structure of the self. A conscious shift occurs as the meaning attached to being lesbian manifests itself in greater satisfaction and an increased sense of happiness.[59] Self-disclosure becomes automatic since few persons at this stage feel a need to remain secretive about their identities.

Within the community of lesbians there is debate about whether everyone ought to eventually arrive at stage six. Some lesbians believe that being open and honest is the only healthy way to live. Those who remain silent are understood to be participating in the perpetuation of negative stereotypes and the lack of broader movements toward justice. Ultimately, however, the choices about disclosure must remain with individual women who know the context of their own particular lives.

Pastoral caregivers can offer sanctuaries for women who want to explore their emerging lesbian identities. At times pastoral care specialists can take the initiative and invite persons to consider a shift in their self-perceptions, encouraging them through the stages described above. However, it is never appropriate to insist that women either move toward self-identification as lesbians or abandon the process. Reminding women that the development of lesbian identities occurs over time and should not be rushed can give women the freedom they need to explore and make appropriate choices for themselves.

Proactive Pastoral Counseling with Emilia and Grace

Grace and Emilia bring to the pastoral counselor both the individual process of identity formation and concerns for their partnership. The four activities and theological themes lifted up earlier in this chapter provide a framework for pastoral care with Emilia and Grace.

Naming and Being Named

The activity of naming and being named appears in Emilia and Grace's partnership. Tensions have arisen in their relationship around the potential of sharing living space. Along with the pragmatic and normal anxieties generated by moving emotionally and physically closer to each other, a core issue may have surfaced. By moving in together, Emilia and Grace are naming themselves as "partners" at a more formal level than ever before. Naturally, questions arise about what that naming of themselves will mean in their collective and individual futures. Chapter 3 deals more explicitly with covenant and partnership, but it is important to recognize here that the movement toward naming themselves as partners is integral to their story.

Naming is central in each individual's story as well. Self-identifying for Emilia, or the naming of herself as lesbian, appears to occur most naturally. Her sense of being created, or born, as a lesbian works positively in affirming her orientation identity. A pastoral counselor can build upon this strength in working with Emilia, relating not only to how she names herself as lesbian but seeking also to understand what it means from her perspective to have been created with this gift. Emilia, to use Cass's developmental frame, is at least in the stage of identity tolerance, if not beyond. To clarify her process, the pastoral caregiver will be interested in hearing more about how Emilia understands herself, with whom she socializes the most, and how she has come to think about being lesbian in the culture. Answers to these types of questions, while not "proving" where she or anyone else is in the identity formation process, at least offer some indicators of Emilia's current self-perception. The question remains as to whether this naming of herself as lesbian gives her internal power to stand the chaos of the moment.

Grace is probably in the late stage of identity confusion or identity comparison. She has not yet come to define herself as lesbian, but she is committed to her current relationship with Emilia. The tension created in sharing a house might indicate that Grace may feel caught between being named or perceived as lesbian and wanting to lean into the next step toward naming her identity as lesbian. The thought of being named by others has created some internal conflict, as shown by Grace's questions that focus on how she will be received by her community of faith. Added to this concern is the complex issue, faced by many women, of making choices about telling children. Being named as a lesbian mother adds another dimension to Grace's identity formation.

Given that Grace and Emilia are in very different places related to naming and being named, the potential for tension in the relationship is high. A pastoral caregiver must work intentionally as Grace and Emilia negotiate their way through a process that raises a number of questions: How long can Emilia be accepting of Grace's unwillingness to name the relationship as lesbian? If Grace ultimately chooses not to name herself as lesbian and shifts back to a heterosexual posture, what will be the impact of such a process on each of them? Or, how might the dynamics between them change if Grace shifts quickly into the next stage of lesbian identity, catching them both by surprise?

Care specialists must proceed slowly, therapeutically joining the relationship without placing undue pressure on Grace to be silent about her questions nor on Emilia to merely stand by and wait for Grace to make up her mind. A pastoral caregiver must work to sustain Grace in her ambivalence and Emilia in her fears about the relationship, without taking sides.

Embracing Sexuality

Sexuality is that broad and encompassing aspect of our lives that touches the human need for connection and intimacy. Sensual and sexual expressions are the most intimate ways to encounter such communion. Being in relationship with another person and experiencing intimacy through loving, physical expressions become powerful moments in sensing God's care. Grace's questions about what God thinks of her loving another woman, or whether God has created her to be lesbian, point toward the weaving together of sexuality and theology in everyday relationships.

As Emilia and Grace name themselves and contemplate what it means to be named by others as lesbian, they will reveal fragments of their perception of sexuality. Recalling that sexuality is more than sexual intercourse, the pastoral counselor will want to listen carefully for references to their understandings of gender, their socialization as women, the differences in how they think persons come to be lesbian, and the manifestation of their love in sensual and sexual experiences.

There may be an opportunity in working with Emilia and Grace, particularly given the questions raised by Grace, to talk candidly about God in relation to sexuality. Does each woman experience God's grace in her creation as a woman? Does their sharing of sensual affection (not only in the physical act of making love) assist them in moving toward wholeness? Do they affirm that God's aliveness is present in their erotic life? Do they feel a sense of communion, not only with each other but with a transcendent Being? Conversations such as these can be filled with richness as pastoral care specialists empower women to embrace their sexuality. Women like Grace and Emilia offer pastoral theologians opportunities to listen anew to what it means to embody God's grace in sexual relationships.

At one level, the issue for Emilia and Grace is not that they are lesbians but that as individuals and as partners they are seeking to integrate their sexuality with other aspects of their identities. At another level, however, Grace and Emilia, like many lesbian women, probably find it difficult to believe that their sexuality as women and as lesbians is an expression of God's goodness.

Connecting Spirituality

Spirituality is often neglected when working with women in lesbian relationships, even in the context of pastoral care and counseling. Connecting spirituality and sexuality in the context of lesbian relationships remains one of the most profound gifts pastoral representatives can bring to their vocations. As caregivers they can provide opportunities for women to connect their orientations, their identities, their emotional lives, their passions, and their spiritual energies to a transcendent and immanent Being.

Integral to spirituality are the passions women bring to their lives and their relationships. This passionate love may be expressed in the erotic life they share together or in the commitments that energize them individually or as partners. Watching carefully for glimmers of passion to surface in conversations with Emilia and Grace, the pastoral counselor can gently guide, confront, and challenge these women to feel the movement of the spirit in their life together. Each woman brings her spiritual experiences into the relationship. Helping each to articulate, value, and affirm that spirituality can be essential in keeping them connected to themselves, to each other, and to their experience of God.

It would be easy to get caught up in this case with helping Grace discern whether she is lesbian. Using the gifts of psychodynamic theories, scientific research, and insights from the social construction theorists, the pastoral caregiver might adequately address the various concerns that Grace has raised. A more meaningful approach to the question of Grace's orientation, however, is to attend to the way she expresses her passions and desires. Listening to both Grace and Emilia identify their passions about life and love provides insight into what it means for each of them to be in love with another woman. At a fundamental level this approach enables the pastoral caregiver to work with the spiritual dimension of their individual lives and their partnership.

There are two specific ways to connect with the spiritual lives of Grace and Emilia. First, Grace has expressed her concern about the response of the community of faith to her relationship with Emilia. While this may be interpreted as a pragmatic concern about what others might think, the pastoral caregiver who can get underneath the surface might discover a spiritual longing for connection to God, self, and others. Where is God's presence felt in the midst of the internal conflicts Grace is experiencing? How does God move in her decisions about her sexual identity and orientation? What impact does the community of faith have on Grace's spiritual life? Emilia has not voiced her spiritual concerns as much as Grace has in this initial conversation, yet it would be naive to think that those concerns are not present in her searching. Helping them explore the connection of their spiritual lives to their relationship and their sexual identities offers Grace and Emilia an opportunity to connect their passions with God.

A final way of connecting spirituality with Grace and Emilia's life is to consider how their church experiences have affected their lives. Both Emilia and Grace have talked about their respective churches from the past or the present. Emilia's detachment from church does not imply that she is not looking for a community where she can be nurtured, challenged, and engaged at a spiritual level. Grace's concern about her church reveals something about the significance of that community in her life. Finding churches that openly affirm their relationship may be difficult and this, in turn, can negatively affect their spirituality. However, there are other avenues for finding communities that seek to nurture their spiritual lives. Connecting with friends or others in alternative communal experiences can be one way of enriching their spiritual lives.

Moving toward
Liberation

Moving from oppression to liberation is a challenging and painful journey. Grace and Emilia, individually and as a partnership, experience oppression in several ways. Women in lesbian relationships encounter biases as women and as lesbians in their families, among their friends, in their churches, and in the culture. Proactive pastoral care seeks to identify oppression and helps to create strategies for moving toward liberation.

Thoughtful reflection about what it is like for Emilia and Grace to be in a lesbian relationship in this culture can evoke feelings of anger, fear, sadness, or shame. Grace's awareness that she may not be accepted by others does not suggest that she is paranoid. Instead, Grace reflects the very real possibility that she may lose friends, the support of her church, or relationships with her children should they know about her relationship. Inviting Emilia to talk about what it has been like for her to be lesbian in this culture can illuminate the risks and genuine fears of being named a lesbian. Simple things like how they imagine their house can demonstrate places of oppression. Will they each have a separate bedroom, one of which is rarely used? Will they "straighten" up the house or remove any sign that they are partners when their families or friends come to visit? Oppression is exhibited in the lack of communal structures that support other more traditional heterosexual marriages.

Moving toward liberation means inviting Grace and Emilia to think about the freedoms they might experience in their lives if the oppression they experience were to be lifted. For example, has oppression become an element in Grace's fears about being named as lesbian? Knowing that life does not become easier when one chooses a lesbian lifestyle sometimes keeps a person from claiming her identity. Oppression may be one of the reasons Emilia has not remained active in her church or it may be present in her mother's inability to totally affirm her.

Freedom from oppression for women like Emilia and Grace invites them to live without fear. Liberation does not necessarily mean that Grace should fully enter into the relationship with Emilia. Her doubts and questions need to be listened to, accepted, and understood. The question is not whether Grace and Emilia ought to spend the rest of their lives together. Instead, the question is how can the pastoral caregiver assist Emilia and Grace to feel empowered to make their choices with integrity and honesty?

This chapter has explored fundamental questions about lesbian identity. The activities of naming and being named, embracing sexuality, connecting spirituality, and moving toward liberation illuminate theological themes that are prevalent in lesbian identity formation. Theoretical conceptualizations from theories in the fields of psychology, science, and the social construction of knowledge provide tools for reflecting with women about their orientations and identities. Affirming that identity formation is a process offers women the freedom to articulate their questions and struggle with choices in relationships. Pastoral caregivers extend genuine respect and care for them as individuals and as women in relationship when they face with them the issues presented in this chapter.

Chapter Three

Covenants of Love, Justice, and Mutuality

Jeanne and Sharon have known each other for almost a year. Since her late high school years Jeanne, who is twenty-three, has had a number of relationships with women. Sharon, twenty-eight, has been in only two significant relationships with women, each lasting about two years. She has dated both women and men and until three years ago described herself as bisexual. Sharon now feels that her lesbian orientation is more true to her self-understandings. The relationships she has with women feel stronger and are more connected to her emotional and spiritual ideals of long-term committed partnerships. Sharon is convinced that Jeanne is the person she wants to share her life with and Jeanne has expressed similar feelings. Last week they found an apartment to rent, and they hope to be in a position to buy a house within a year. Since their second-month anniversary they have moved steadily toward an exclusive relationship, agreeing not to go out with other women. They describe few places of tension in their relationship and seem to agree with each other on almost everything.

Recently Sharon and Jeanne attended a "holy union" for two of their gay men friends. This experience prompted them to think about having a service before moving into their apartment next month. A few of their lesbian friends have actively discouraged them from having a service, suggesting that it is only a way for them to make believe that they are "married" in a culture that does not allow them such a privilege.

Jeanne and Sharon place a call to the pastor of the church they attend, hoping to find someone to assist them in sorting through the questions raised by their friends. As the time for the appointment approaches, the pastor wonders exactly how to structure the conversation with Sharon and Jeanne. Never having counseled women who want a holy union service, the pastoral caregiver is not sure how to proceed. Is this like any other "pre-marital counseling" appointment, or is there something distinctive about the request by Jeanne and Sharon? What does it mean to work with women who want to formalize their relationship? Are these relationships really any different from marriages? What if they want the minister to officiate at the service but the denomination does not condone such practices? The pastoral care specialist is aware that not only do women in lesbian relationships lack role models but pastoral caregivers who counsel women or who participate in holy union services have few role models as well.

There is something distinct about working with women in lesbian relationships. Treating women who love women as if their situations are the same as every other marital relationship is not helpful. This chapter addresses three elements to consider in pastoral counseling with women in lesbian relationships. First, the cultural and theological symbolisms attached to relationships that extend over time are significant. Normally in the church the language of marriage is used to talk about these kinds of relationships. However, in lesbian relationships the concept of marriage may not be as helpful as the concepts of covenant and partnership. While the symbols of marriage and covenant are not foreign to each other, to assume that marriage can be the paradigm for lesbian partnerships misses the unique issues that women bring to pastoral care.

Second, love, justice, and mutuality are the normative qualities that can guide the formation and development of long-term committed relationships between women. Exploring these themes in the context of the Judeo-Christian community provides pastoral caregivers with a framework for counseling women in lesbian relationships.

Third, lesbian partnerships, not unlike other relationships, move through various stages. Pastoral caregivers who can articulate these seasons in relationships can support women who love women by offering them a possible structure for understanding their experiences. Heterosexual couples often have families, friends, and churches with whom they can celebrate their marriages or mourn their losses of relationships. But, because of the heterosexism in the culture and in religious organizations, many women in lesbian relationships do not have the same privilege. There are few structures for talking openly about lesbian experiences. A concept of seasons in partnerships enables pastoral counselors to be aware of how best to care for women in relationships.

Returning to the story of Jeanne and Sharon illuminates the discussion of covenantal partnership in this chapter. Proactive pastoral caregivers not only welcome the opportunity to work with lesbians but also are proactive in encouraging families, churches, and denominations to talk openly about what it means for women to enter into covenants and partnerships.

Marriages and Covenants:
The Uniqueness of Lesbian Partnerships

Jeanne, Sharon, and their friends represent the diversity of perspectives within the community of women who love women. These perspectives range from that of those who desire to formalize their relationship through holy unions to those who adamantly oppose such services. The lesbian community does not agree about holy unions, their meanings, or their values. Questions arise in various ways: Would the legalization of marriage for lesbian partnerships encourage greater justice and liberation for lesbians as well as for people in other nontraditional relationships? Is the desire to participate in a service of commitment merely an attempt to fit into normative structures for relationships? Why is it important for some women to find ministers to do holy union services when the church, for the most part, is not supportive of their relationships? What does it mean that women in nontraditional relationships participate in conventional forms of being "bound" to one another and refer to themselves as being married? Do lesbian partnerships challenge the status quo of traditional heterosexual marriages and offer a new vision for relating in meaningful ways?

Marriage is the model most involved in conversations about holy unions and covenant services. The internalization of marriage as an "idea" and an "ideal" occurs in the psyches and souls of persons through complex socialization processes. Concepts about marriage are transmitted through cultural institutions (legal systems, schools, churches) and through individual family environments. The institutionalization of marriage raises questions about what is culturally normative, how relationships are formed and maintained, and how meaning is conveyed from one generation to the next. Lesbian partnerships differ from traditional heterosexual marriages. At least four difficulties arise in using the language and imagery of marriage as a symbol for lesbian relationships.

First, marriage has its historical roots in economic, social, and political contexts. Marriage did not begin as a romantic notion about two persons falling in love and committing themselves to one another because of the depth of their love. Recent works of John Boswell, Gerda Lerner, and others remind readers that the origins of marriage are neither theological nor romantic.[1] Lerner argues that "[t]he appropriation by men of women's sexual and reproductive capacity occurred *prior* to the formation of private property and class society. Its commodification lies, in fact, at the foundation of private property."[2] Class and property issues were resolved on the ability of women to reproduce. Romance was not as important as producing boy children who could continue the lineage. The legalization of marriage was based upon the need to protect men's property rights, including their ownership of the sexuality of women and children.[3]

Marriage was and continues to be, in part, legally binding. Lesbians and gay men who desire the legalization of marriage as an option for their relationships are acutely aware of the economic and legal advantages of being married. As nonmarried partners they face particular challenges in a culture that offers preference to legally married spouses. Women who love women want to participate in structures that support their relationships. There is little doubt, for example, that women who struggle financially would be helped by the cultural and social benefits of legal marriage (e.g., access to family health insurance, joint applications to purchase a new home, not having to fear loss of custody of children simply because of being lesbian). At the same time, participation in the legal structures of marriage gives states power in the relationship that not all lesbians want.[4] For example, women may not want to be legally bound in ways that make transitions out of relationships impossible without the assistance of a court or legal system.

A second difficulty with marriage as a paradigm for lesbian long-term relationships rests in its patriarchal history and structure. As noted above, a significant reason for establishing marriage as a legal institution was protection of the rights of men. Lerner traces the history of male dominance and its internalization in cultural symbols such as marriage. She reminds readers that "[t]he first gender-defined social role for women was to be those who were exchanged in marriage transactions. The obverse gender role for men was to be those who did the exchanging or who defined the terms of the exchanges."[5] Separating the history of marriage as a system to preserve male property rights from subtle, patriarchal oppression in contemporary culture is difficult, at best. There are women who maintain that the cultural institution of marriage may not be redeemable. Patriarchal structures continue to manifest themselves in traditional marriages through male-dominated households, disparaging views of women who work outside the home, the shortage of resources for adequate childcare for working mothers, and traditional notions about the role of women and men in family life.

Lesbian relationships, particularly for women who seek to be liberated from patriarchal structures, are based on notions of equality and mutuality. Interpreting lesbian partnerships as marriages reinforces, at least at the unconscious level, more patriarchal and hierarchical ways of relating. Many of the eloquent articles supporting the legalization of gay marriages are written by men who do not struggle with patriarchy in the same way that women do. The vast majority of writers who question marriage as a liberating option are women. The foundation of their concern is the traditional patriarchal understandings of marriage.[6] Lesbians are women who have witnessed the underside of patriarchy and who seek for new ways of being in relationship.

A third difficulty with the image of marriage has to do with the assumption that heterosexuality is necessary for healthy relationships. Patricia Jung and Ralph Smith argue that the heterosexism attached to the reading of the creation stories and a number of other biblical texts reinforces the belief that the best relationships are those consisting of one man and one woman.[7] It is as if one gender, without the other, cannot be whole. Theological and cultural understandings of marriage have embodied this conceptual framework in ways that are not helpful for women in lesbian relationships. Most lesbians can attest to the numerous times people have suggested to them that their relationships are not whole because men are not present.

The ideal of marriage is so intimately connected with what it means to be a healthy person that it is almost impossible for many in our culture to envision a healthy person who is not married—particularly if that person has made a *choice* not to marry. For example, a bias is often held against women who are single and not in a long-term committed relationship. Many single persons are viewed by others as being unhappy and less than whole. The belief that all healthy women yearn for and choose intimate relationships with men is directly challenged by lesbian partners. Many lesbians do relate to men, but they find their most meaningful relationships with women.

Finally, marriage has been intimately linked to understandings of procreation and the perpetuation of the family. The Western cultural norm is that a woman marries a man and, if possible, they have children. Bringing children into the world becomes a primary expectation within and about the marriage. Is procreation the purpose of marriage? The church has institutionalized erotic love through its preoccupation with childbearing. The pleasure and fullness of genital and sexual activity have been replaced by concerns about procreation and generativity. Perhaps this is not as much a question about marriage as about perceptions of sexuality.[8] Cultural pressure to have children is felt not only by lesbian partners, but by heterosexual couples who either cannot conceive or choose not to.

Many lesbian partnerships are blessed with children, yet procreation does not as clearly define the purpose of the relationship as it does for some heterosexual marriages. "Family" has a broader connotation for the lesbian community. Kath Weston, in an anthropological study of lesbians, gays, and their families, notes that "discussions of gay families pictured kinship as an *extension* of friendship."[9] Women in lesbian relationships often refer to their close and intimate lesbian and gay male friends as brothers and sisters. A common vernacular among lesbian and gay persons is to refer to one another as "family."

Families of choice are not marked by traditional boundaries or legal definitions, nor are they limited to sexual partners or lovers. Women in lesbian relationships understand their families of choice to include those who are close and intimate friends. Families can include persons who do not share the same living spaces, asexual relationships (the stereotyped Boston marriage), women who are legally married to men and have a lesbian lover and/or an emotional relationship with a woman, or ex-partners who remain close friends and share common experiences after separating.[10]

Given these four difficulties with the symbol of marriage, the preferred language in this book is lesbian relationships, covenants, or partnerships. Some pastoral care specialists try to treat lesbian partners as if they were straight couples who differ only in the way they make love to each other. This misses the subtle ways in which women in lesbian relationships can never be integrated into traditional understandings of heterosexual marriage. Valuing lesbian partners and their extended concept of family is extremely important; utilizing the trappings of marriage can be destructive.

The phrase "women in lesbian relationships" or "lesbian partners" has been used in this book rather than "lesbian couples." This is done as an intentional reminder that women who share their lives are not the same as a man and woman who fall in love, get married, and create a heterosexual family. Heterosexual couples have social structures, including the support of the church, through which they can affirm their relationships. Women who love women rarely have the benefit of pastoral care specialists who honor and value their lesbian relationships. Many women refer to themselves as lesbian couples or they talk about being married, and hearing and honoring their language is important. Pastoral caregivers are most helpful, however, when they challenge themselves to understand what women are trying to convey by choosing that language. Offering women new perspectives and, perhaps, new language can contribute to their ongoing process of moving toward liberation.

Covenants

Theological meanings of covenant have always been pivotal to Judeo-Christian understandings of significant relationships. Hence, it is not incidental that notions of covenant inform the conversations between pastoral caregivers and women in lesbian relationships.[11]

The notion of covenant is often confused with understandings of contract. In the cultural milieu of social obligations, legal terms, and litigation many persons seem to be more comfortable discussing the binding of contracts than reflecting upon the significance of covenant from a pastoral theological perspective. For example, pastoral care specialists often verbalize the contracts necessary for good therapy, but they don't always reflect as clearly upon the covenantal qualities that create the healing environment for care and counseling. Paul F. Palmer differentiates between contract and covenant:

> Covenant (*foedus*) is as expansive and as all-embracing as contract is restrictive and limiting. From the root word *fidus* and the verb form *fidere*, which means to trust, to have faith in, to entrust oneself to another, a covenant is seen as a relationship of mutual trust and fidelity (*fides*). . . . Contracts can be broken by mutual agreement, by failure to live up to the terms of the contract, by civil intervention. Covenants are not broken; they are violated when there is a breach of faith on the part of either or both of the covenanters.[12]

Palmer points out that contracts are mutual agreements about things and property, such as contracting for someone's services. Covenants, however, are established in the context of human relationships. Contracts are broken when one party does not live up to the negotiated terms, hence invalidating the contract. Because of their relational base, when covenants are violated, the relationship itself suffers.

Covenants are established not on the basis of legal conditions but on the basis of faith and trust in the relationship.[13] This is significant when considering long-term covenantal partnerships with women in lesbian relationships. Women who love women do not enter into formal structures supported and maintained by social and legal contracts. Instead, lesbian partners have the opportunity to deal intentionally with what it means to form covenantal partnerships, in part because they have fewer legal parameters around which to structure their relationships.

Covenants formed in the context of ancient Israel (but not unique to that community of faith) were marked by a number of components. These provided the lens through which the Israelites viewed their relationship with God.[14] Four elements from antiquity, when appropriated by pastoral care specialists, can inform the covenantal partnerships of lesbian relationships.

First, a covenant articulated the promises made by the participants in the relationship. Delbert Hillers suggests that in antiquity covenants were entered into by means of "an oath by each member of the community, administered and renewed in the most formal way possible."[15] Making the conscious decision to enter into an oath illuminated the importance of freedom and choice on the part of the people in their relationship with God. As one author notes, in the ancient Mosaic covenant, "the covenant ceremony itself was an invitation to decision."[16] Hence, the promises, intentions, and resulting consequences of violating the covenant were established on the basis of freedom and choice. For example, in the Mosaic covenant, both God and Moses acknowledged their intentions in the relationship, including the curses and blessings of maintaining or violating the covenant.

As women enter lesbian partnerships, they choose the principles that will guide their relationships. These decisions, however, are often made at an unconscious level and may not be verbalized in a conscious and forthright manner. Since covenants serve to articulate the intentions of each participant in the relationship, it is vital that they be voiced in some intentional way. Many women desire opportunities to talk about their relationships, their faith, and their commitments. However, because of the lack of formal opportunities for such talk, they may fail to adequately discuss the intentions or obligations they expect from each other. Often the result is that assumptions about relationships rest under the surface until crises or misunderstandings arise. Proactive pastoral caregivers can offer women the opportunity to voice the qualities they want to have in their relationships, moving assumptions into conscious awareness.

A second aspect of ancient covenants was their communal nature. Historically, covenants were established not between individuals but between persons and communities. For example, God's covenant was not just with Moses but with the community of which Moses was a part. This, again, is significant for women in lesbian partnerships. Women in lesbian relationships participate in the broader communities of which they are a part. At times these communities may be confined to other lesbians or gay men who share their visions. However, for many women there is a genuine desire to have their partnership recognized in their community of faith, either formally or informally. Hence, they seek out pastors and churches who can support their relationships. Unfortunately, finding supportive communities of faith happens far less frequently than should be the case.

The communal nature of covenants is experienced in lesbian relationships as primary relationships between women are nurtured and developed in the networks of friendships and families. At the same time, lesbian partnerships by their mere existence challenge the structures of church and society. The presence of two women who appear to be partners within a local church cannot be ignored, even when the women may choose not to be too revealing about the nature of their relationship. The partnership of the women is probably acknowledged by many within the congregation at some deep, internal level, thereby confronting traditional ways of approaching relationships. Women in relationship with each other do not live isolated lives; they affect those around them in subtle and sometimes radical ways. Pastoral care specialists would do well to recognize that even when women do not openly acknowledge their relationship, their presence reminds persons of the communal nature of covenants.

Third, covenants of antiquity provided for "periodic renewal" as participants were reminded about the meaning and importance of the covenant through liturgical or celebrative events. The Hebrew scriptures rehearsed the history of their covenants over and over again, reminding the people of Israel about their relationship with God.[17] Liturgies and celebrations became ritual opportunities for reexamination and renewal of the ancient covenants.

Usually women in lesbian relationships do not have public events to celebrate their covenants. Important stages in their lives may be celebrated privately, but rarely are there opportunities for women to invite others to join them. While heterosexual couples have people who remind them on their anniversaries about having been at their wedding, there are few such persons for women in lesbian partnerships. Those who formalize their relationship with a ritual service, or holy union, may have a date they identify as an "anniversary." However, rarely is this a date that is marked on their families' calendars.

Women who do not have an anniversary date need other ways to be reminded about their covenants. Women can often remember many dates such as their first meeting, the first time they spent the night together, the first time they pulled together in a crisis to care for their family, or the setting up of a common household. Inquiring about those moments that women recognize in their relationships as being important can provide the pastoral care specialist with a sense of how a particular covenant has been developed. Simultaneously the telling of the stories and their being heard and valued by caregivers can serve to be opportunities of "periodic renewal" for the partnership, reminding women about the meaning and importance of their covenants.

Finally, covenants are not static, but dynamic and fluid. Few covenants remain the same over time. Historically it is possible to see shifts in the covenants of antiquity by reading the biblical texts. Covenants change as circumstances and relationships evolve. In an article on families, Walter Brueggemann points out that relationships are places where people learn about "covenant-making, covenant-keeping, covenant-breaking, and covenant-renewing."[18] Illustrative of this fluid understanding are the covenants formed between children and parents. The boundaries, expectations, and promises made between young children and their parents are different from those established between adult children who care for their elderly parents.

Since relationships are dynamic rather than rigid and static, covenants made between women have a fluid quality. Over time women discover that some patterns in their relationships do not work for various reasons. Established systems do not easily give way to new ones; energy and work are required to reshape a former way of relating. Covenants must be made and kept with full knowledge that they may also be fractured. Women often need assistance in discerning how to reshape their covenants so that they reflect the commitments and qualities they desire most in their relationships. Pastoral caregivers who invite women to reflect upon the foundations of their values, commitments, and hopes also encourage women to remember that their covenants are dynamic and fluid rather than static.

Qualities in
Covenantal Partnerships

The relational qualities of love, justice, and mutuality provide the foundation for covenantal partnerships. Women who love women do not (and at the moment cannot) depend upon legal parameters or contractual agreements to structure their relationships. Pastoral care specialists are most helpful when they engage women in partnership to reflect upon the meanings of love, justice, and mutuality in their relationships.

Love

Pondering the meaning of love in covenantal relationships is not, by any stretch of the imagination, a new topic for consideration. As Daniel Day Williams notes in his classic, *The Spirit and Forms of Love*, "there is no one way to express the meaning of love in the Christian faith."[19] However, the question for this book is how the love expressed between two women might be distinctive in lesbian partnerships. Four issues are significant in examining the presence of love between women.

First, love is reflected in the depth of the friendships women have with one another. Mary Hunt, in her theo-ethical exploration of women's friendships, notes the importance of such bonds between women. She lifts up the passion of women's friendships by suggesting that there is a "fierce tenderness" present in these relationships.

> I call friendships "fierce" because of the intensity of attention. It can be hard to be known so well, to be understood and transparent to friends who pay attention. Likewise, we all crave the tenderness that only those who love us can offer. Tenderness does not affect the ferocity, but it is the quality of care and nurture that only friends share. Of course a care giver can be tender in touch, but only friends are tender in feeling.[20]

Hunt goes on to suggest that this fierce tenderness provides some of the core ethical perspectives that can guide relationships not only between friends but between lovers and, ultimately, between communities. Love, one component of women's friendships, reflects "an orientation toward the world as if my friend and I were more united than separated, more at one among the many than separate and alone."[21] In the lesbian community, women often reflect this sentiment of being more united than separated by remaining friends even after the intensity of a physical or sexual relationship is over.

Feminist object relations theorists, along with others in women's studies, have illuminated the significance of women's ways of relating to one another. The work of theoreticians like Nancy Chodorow, Luise Eichenbaum, and Susie Orbach make it clear that women develop relationships with one another differently than they develop their relationships with men. While Chodorow disagrees with Eichenbaum and Orbach about the specificity of these differences, they all agree that women are connected with one another in particularly passionate ways.[22]

The fact that women are most often primary caretakers and mothering figures creates a distinct bond and intensity that appears later in women's friendships. Chodorow believes that women have more flexible ego boundaries than men have and are, therefore, able to develop more breadth in their ways of relating to others. The asymmetrical pattern established as men father and women mother (often with men being more distant and women more connected) results in greater attention by women to relatedness, such as mothers and their girl children who remain connected in significant ways throughout their lives. Women, who are usually not valued for being mothers or for their relational qualities, develop a lower sense of self-esteem.[23] Eichenbaum and Orbach agree that women and men develop relational skills in distinct ways, but they suggest that the malleability of boundaries for women leads to less clarity than men have about their sense of differentiation as a self. At the same time, women appear to have more clarity than men have about relatedness and more intense feelings about other women. While there are significant differences between the theoretical perspectives of Chodorow and of Eichenbaum and Orbach, they all suggest that women's relationships with one another are filled with a kind of intensity and relational connection that is not always apparent in male-female or in gay male relationships.

The intensity that feminist object relations theorists attribute to women's friendships is especially apparent when difficulties and disagreements arise between women.[24] Expecting relatedness, unity, and connection with each other because women are more alike than not alike, women appear to be deeply sensitive to the difficulties, disappointments, and anxieties that arise as they discover their differences and their humanness.[25] Women often experience discomfort when there is conflict and difference in the way they express their intimacy and affection. Pastoral caregivers who frame the intensity of lesbian relationships in ways that are congruent with the depth of genuine love and care of women's friendships can assist lesbian partners in developing relationships that are guided by an enduring love that withstands differences.

A second issue, sexuality, is a vital component of love between women. While lesbian partnerships contain strong elements of friendship, there is more to the relationship than platonic connections. Carter Heyward talks about "erotic friendship" as shaping the content of ethics in relationships. Building upon her vision of the erotic as "the sacred/godly basis of our capacity to participate in mutually empowering relationships," Heyward is particularly insightful about the importance and power of eros in the context of significant relationships.[26] Lesbian partnerships include the power of not only friendship but also erotic love. The sexual aspect of partnership should not be overlooked, just as it should not be the exclusive focus of pastoral counseling.

In recent studies on the sexual lives of women and men in a variety of relationships, respondents suggested that women in lesbian relationships have, perhaps, the lowest frequency level of sexual intimacy.[27] This should not be interpreted to mean that lesbians are not interested in sexual intimacy. However, at least two realities converge to suggest that women in lesbian relationships experience sexual intimacy in a manner different from that experienced in other kinds of relationships.

First, women in lesbian relationships may define the sexual nature of their lives in ways that cannot be quantified by researchers asking specifically about sexual intercourse. Many women enjoy hugging, cuddling, kissing, and stroking one another without the need for climax or penetration. The cultural definition of sexual intercourse is typically based on a model of male-to-female penetration, which is inappropriate for understanding sexual lesbian relationships. Hence, the response to questions about sexual frequency may say more about the cultural definitions of sex than about a lack of sexuality in lesbian partnerships. According to psychologist Margaret Nichols,

> some research suggests that, overall, lesbians may be more sexually responsive and more satisfied with the sex they do have than are heterosexual women. . . . Masters and Johnson speculate that the sexual techniques of lesbians, which tend to be sensuous, less genitally and orgasm focused, and less oriented to vaginal penetration, are generally more suited to the sexual needs of women than is heterosexual sexual activity.[28]

Second, women bring different internalizations about sexuality into their relationships. The engendering of women in our culture is often connected with particular images about sexuality. For example, many women learn that they should not be assertive in asking that their needs be met, that men's sexual needs are to be met before women's, or that they are to be receptive and passive in expressing their sexuality. In the case of survivors of sexual abuse, women often internalize beliefs that their sexual feelings are bad or that other persons are always more powerful than they are in relationships. The result is that women may initiate sexual intimacy with one another at a lower frequency than do men and women in traditional heterosexual relationships. Lesbian women may take less sexual initiative in their relationships, not because sex is unimportant, but because their relationships have been engendered in ways that do not foster sexual expression.[29] Caring sexual love between lesbians may appear in ways that seem curious to those who do not seriously consider the socialization and internalization processes in women's development.

The area of sexual intimacy is, perhaps, one of the most misunderstood by those who work with women in lesbian partnerships. Women who love women cannot be identified only by their sexual expressions of love, nor are women who love women denying their sexuality because they engage in sexual intercourse less often. Instead, women in lesbian relationships express their sexuality with one another in ways that may be different from cultural norms or expectations. The culture's heterosexism creeps into the pastoral care context through a denial of the power of sexual intimacy in lesbian relationships or in an overvaluing of the erotic love expressed between two women. Virginia Ramey Mollenkott's warning to her readers is a valuable reminder to pastoral care specialists: "[I]t is vital that we never allow society's erotophobia to rob us of our sensuous spirituality."[30] Sexuality is vital in the covenants of lesbian partnerships. Pastoral caregivers must remain open to different expressions of sexuality and love.

A third component of love is its ability to provide a sense of security in covenantal relationships. To be secure does not mean that persons can rest assured that no tensions, anxieties, or fears will exist in their relationships. Security does, however, emerge in relationships in two instrumental ways. First, there is security in the experience of being loved. The internal feeling of safety and assurance when a person feels the intimacy of being cared for, especially when that love is expressed with an unconditional quality, is undeniably present in lesbian relationships.

A second way persons experience security is related to how lesbians experience the culture around them. To have a partner means that a person can rest assured that she does not have to face the prejudice and biases of the world alone. The fact that women choose to enter into lesbian relationships despite the oppression they face within the church and culture should not be minimized. Women continue to choose one another and that, in itself, is significant. The power of love, Daniel Day Williams wrote, "is the security which it gives in our relations to one another. . . . It is the reality to which we cling in a broken, confused and threatening existence. It is the root of life, and its binding power."[31]

Choosing to covenant with another conveys a sense of security. Pepper Schwartz suggests that the freedom of choice persons have in their primary relationship contributes to the power of the friendship at the base of those relationships. Relationships are at their best when they are grounded in peer friendships and in the intentional process of choosing one another as friends.

> Friends choose each other repeatedly during the lifetime of a relationship. Nothing but their affection for each other and their acceptance of

the nature of their relationship keeps them together. . . . To qualify as a
real friendship spouses would choose each other for the sheer joy of each
other's company.[32]

It is the sense of choosing each other, in spite of the lack of support from
communities, families, friends, legal systems, or anything else, that keeps
some lesbian partnerships alive and vital. Choosing each other allows the
partnership to withstand the kind of chaos and tension that is present in
many human relationships. A significant point in covenantal partnerships occurs when women settle into trusting that together they will survive whatever conflict and chaos emerges from inside or from outside the relationship.

Expecting partnerships to provide security from an outside world can
put tremendous pressure upon the relationships. There are those who suggest that women in lesbian relationships are too clingy or too attached to
each other. Some partners, as in many relationships, are overly enmeshed
in the other's life. However, more often what persons are observing from
the outside is the need for lesbian partners to depend upon each other in
ways that others in the culture may not experience. Significant stress can
be put on relationships if families of origin are not supportive of lesbian
partnerships, or if careers are at stake because women choose to love other
women. Instead of turning to others (families, friends, colleagues, church
pastors) who may reject them because of their lesbian relationships, women
sometimes turn inward to the partnership and depend upon each other to
meet too many of their friendship and intimacy needs. The security of being loved and cared for in partnerships ought not to make women turn inward; rather, security within the partnership ought to give women enough
strength to reach out to others as well.

The ability to reach out to others relates, finally, to the fourth component of love in a covenantal partnership. Love expressed between women
should not be a love that turns inward on itself, but a love that fosters in
persons the energy it takes to move outward into the broader community
and the world. Love is more than feeling close to someone. Genuine
covenantal love is reflected not only in the partnerships themselves but in
the relationships women have with extended families, friends, and communities of faith. Love, according to Larry Graham,

> is the generous embodied giving and receiving on behalf of the welfare
> of individual persons and the larger social communities comprising
> them. It extends to include a benevolent reciprocal engagement with na-
> ture. Love is increased when persons move from estrangement and
> disharmony with themselves, one another, and nature, to an expanding
> and open communion and creativity within and among themselves.[33]

This expansive aspect of lesbian partnerships can engage women in
working for a more just world. It is not unusual to find lesbians who are in-

volved in the fight for social justice, working with persons living with AIDS, or in other action-oriented movements of society. Women's music, art, and other media often reflect the genuine outreach of lesbians beyond their partnership to the broader structures of community. Covenants that invite women to reach out beyond themselves are those that reflect the quality of love apparent in vital lesbian partnerships. A faithful covenant for women in lesbian partnerships works for a more loving society, not only for love in their primary relationships.

Justice

Many feminist theologians, pastoral theologians, and sexual theologians who write about sexuality, and ethics note the connection between love, sexuality, and justice.[34] Women who love women bring this matter to the foreground with particular clarity since lesbians and gay men are so often victims of sexualized injustice. There are many ways of defining justice, each dependent upon particular contexts.[35] Larry Graham, in his psychosystemic approach to pastoral theology, articulates a definition of justice that is not limited to relationships between two persons: "Justice is a corollary of love, inasmuch as it is principally directed to right relations between persons and the various components of their worlds."[36] For purposes of this book, justice is defined as the building of right relations between persons and communities where there is shared power, honest and open communication, and connection with others outside the primary relationship. A look at each of these components of justice clarifies what it means to offer pastoral care to women in covenantal partnerships.

First, right relations must exist between the two women involved in the primary covenant. Justice requires intentionality and struggle as the qualities of "[s]hared power, shared opportunity, and shared rewards" are embodied in the partnership.[37] When power, opportunity, and rewards are equally accessible to both persons in the relationship, the resulting covenant is based on careful considerations of each other. Relationships based on extreme differentials in power create inequities and imbalances that diminish one or both of the persons in the relationship.

In her work on peer relationships, Pepper Schwartz points out the harm that hierarchy can cause in a primary relationship. When one person in the relationship has more power to make choices or achieve goals or dominates the other, both persons in the relationship suffer. The less powerful person suffers because she is not able to actively pursue her choices or be proactive on her own behalf. She stands the most to lose in the relationship. However, the more powerful one also suffers because she may be unaware of the damage produced in the other, or because of feelings she may carry of being overly responsible for particular aspects of the relationship. The more powerful partner cuts herself off from having a relationship with an equal partner. The result is that the less dominant woman feeds the emotional life of the woman with more power in the relationship, but both lose in the end. Neither person gets to experience the fullness of the relationship, or the fullness of being in control of her own life in ways that are optimal for solid partnerships.[38]

Relationships built on inequity cannot be true partnerships since both persons do not have equal access to emotional, physical, or financial resources. One of the defining qualities of friendships, according to Hunt, is shared power and "the ability to make choices for ourselves, for our dependent children, and with our community."[39] Pastoral counselors working with women in lesbian relationships should address clearly and explicitly the balance of power in these partnerships. Covenants that have the quality of partnership are ones in which there is empowerment of both women in ways that make each one more capable of acting on her own behalf.

It would be naive to think that, simply because lesbian partnerships consist of two women, issues of power are not present. While women may be more attuned than men to thinking in terms of equity and shared power, the reality is that few relationships of any kind are structured from their inception around norms of justice, equality, and mutuality. The hallmark of lesbian relationships that endure and provide both persons in the relationship with a qualitative partnership is a conscious choice to balance the power in their relationships.

A second component of justice is the presence of attitudes such as honesty, openness, courage, and fortitude. The more direct and open the communication between women in relationships, the more potential there is for the creation of right relating. This does not mean that good lesbian partnerships lack conflicts and struggles. Instead, justice requires that honesty and integrity in the midst of conflict be the hallmarks of right relationships. Where there is an openness and willingness to work through issues, there is also an awareness of the need for direct confrontation in a loving and caring fashion.[40]

In meaningful relationships the partners must confront any imbalances of power that were established early in the relationship. Such challenges can become testing grounds for the vitality and courage present in the partnership. Feminist psychiatrist Jean Baker Miller notes that most women fear and avoid confrontations, particularly about issues of power. Given the cultural context in which women are engendered, Miller claims, many women experience an internal fear that they will be seen as selfish if they raise concerns that potentially can create conflict. Not only the fear of being misunderstood but also the accompanying fears of destroying the relationship or being abandoned as a result of confrontation keep women from directly voicing their concerns.[41] This supports Schwartz's observation that partners "attempt to defuse anger over such inequality in two ways.

First, they minimize the impact of hierarchy by making it appear situational. . . . Second, hierarchy is softened by leading parallel lives."[42] Women may avoid dealing honestly with inequities in power by either pretending the inequities are not that important or by finding other places outside the relationship where they experience a sense of power.

Given the intensity of relationships between women, it is particularly important that pastoral care specialists probe the presence of power and powerlessness in lesbian partnerships. At times conflicts overwhelm those within the relationship and they are unable, or unwilling, to conceive of creating new ways of mutually relating. The potential for passionate conflict is apparent, and women need pastoral care specialists who are willing to work with them on communicating in more direct and honest ways. The fluid nature of the covenantal framework allows women in lesbian partnerships to change their ways of relating without having to abandon the relationship. Pastoral caregivers can provide opportunities for women to reflect upon whatever injustices are present in their relationships, inviting them to establish new covenants based upon more mutual ways of relating to each other.

The third component of justice points beyond primary relationships and pursues right relating in other segments of society. Graham notes that "[j]ustice further specifies the quality of embodied love in both personal relationships and in the more impersonal dimensions of organized social life."[43] Justice is not only about how two women in primary relationship share their senses of power but about how they participate in creating just relationships in the world as well. As women who love women pattern their relationships on shared power, openness, and honesty, they also provide a model for the broader community in its pursuit of just ways of relating.

What Graham calls the "impersonal dimensions of organized social life" surround women in lesbian partnerships. The internalization of cultural homophobia in women results in negative self-images and a poorer quality of life than would be the case were their relationships structured around heterosexual norms. Injustices occur at internal levels as women constantly have to remind themselves that they are created in the image of God in the same manner as are any of their neighbors. The internal resources required to face a culture or those churches and institutions that are less than open to their relationships takes its toll on the energy they have to engage meaningfully in other aspects of their lives. Many women in lesbian partnerships are aware of the external structures that prevent them from pursuing an ordinary way of living in neighborhoods, in churches, or in the society.

Pastoral caregivers who recognize the external structures that lead to injustices for lesbian partners can assist women in identifying the costs they pay for living their lives as lesbians. Naming these injustices invites women in lesbian covenants to examine carefully how external realities participate in their oppression, and to draw connections between their experiences and those of others who are marginalized in the culture. The most prophetic pastoral care specialists are those who not only identify the injustices that particular women experience but who also invite lesbian partnerships to work for justice in a broader context. If the energy is available, covenantal lesbian partnerships can work toward changing social and systemic injustice not only to achieve a better quality of life for their partnerships but also to work on behalf of others who suffer injustices.

Mutuality

Covenants of partnership embody mutuality by asserting that, in the context of relationships, there are reciprocal ways of holding each other. Mutuality does not mean that everyone brings the same gifts and graces to the partnership. To be mutual means that each woman carries her partner's best interests and concerns at heart. Mutual accountability in structuring, maintaining, and nurturing covenants of partnership suggests that each individual is responsible for the whole. Heyward defines mutuality as "sharing power in such a way that each participant in the relationship is called forth more fully into becoming who she is—a whole person, with integrity."[44] Mutuality, like love and justice, is formed in the context of primary relationships, yet connects to broader community structures.

According to Jung and Smith, partnerships are also formed around expressions of mutual vulnerability. Relationships that mature around the qualities of covenantal partnership exhibit openness and honesty as women share feelings, dreams, hopes, and pains. As in all relationships, there are times when the covenant is violated, either intentionally or unintentionally. Mutuality in relationships means that women accept that each person in the partnership will, at some point, be hurt by the other and each will cause pain. In mutual partnerships, "[t]he possibility for creating both sorrow and joy is . . . intensified."[45] However, even when persons experience hurt in partnerships, their expectation of mutual honesty and accountability ought to encourage them to be open and forthright with each other. Mutual vulnerability requires mutual accountability.

One place of mutual accountability is how partnerships define the boundaries of their relationships. In the lesbian and gay community, the meaning of monogamy and fidelity is questioned intensely. Monogamy and fidelity have traditionally been defined by the heterosexual community as sexual faithfulness to one's primary relationship. However, in the lesbian and gay communities it is seen as important not to simply employ the heterosexist definition of fidelity in relation to lesbian covenantal partnerships. Instead, fidelity in lesbian relationships centers on how women covenant mutually about the boundaries of their external friendships, accepting responsibility and accountability for maintaining clarity about the agreed-upon emotional and sexual perimeters for relationships with others. Arriving at mutual meanings of fidelity should not be confined to discussions about sexual activity, for as previously suggested, sexuality has a broader interpretation in the context of lesbian relationships.

While nonmonogamy for lesbians can be defined as "a form of intimacy in which a woman concurrently engages in sexual and emotional relationships with more than one woman lover,"[46] mutual fidelity honestly recognizes emotional and physical connections with persons outside the relationship. There are those within the Judeo-Christian community who argue that lesbian partnerships reflect the moral and ethical norms of long-term committed relationships only when they are monogamous, specifically in emotional and sexual expressions. Jung and Smith argue, for example, that one of the benchmarks of partnerships that are congruent with Judeo-Christian ethical norms ought to be their "permanence and exclusivity."[47] Hence, they argue that sexual and emotional monogamy in relationships is an important component of the ethical and moral choices lesbians should make.

Others, however, seem less convinced that monogamy, particularly sexual monogamy, is the cornerstone of healthy and faithful covenantal partnerships. Indeed, many lesbian and gay authors suggest that defining monogamy is difficult in same-sex relationships because of the cultural assumptions about what sex actually is. Does monogamy mean that women friends cannot hold hands with each other or hold each other in bed? Or does monogamy refer only to more active sexual intercourse? Defining monogamy in lesbian relationships is distinct from defining it in the context of heterosexual norms.

Some lesbian and gay writers have been more vehement in their confrontation of monogamy, suggesting it to be a heterosexist adaptation in lesbian partnerships. This has been particularly true in the literature written by gay men and radical feminist lesbians. Their argument is constructed along two lines. First, radical feminists note that monogamy was originally intended to protect the economic and legal rights of males, particularly guaranteeing that a "legitimate" father could be identified for the purpose of clarifying property rights and other legal powers passed on to his heirs.[48] Second, gay men often argue that socialization means that women and men have differing understandings of monogamy. J. Michael Clark suggests that expectations in men "to seek sexual variety and to downplay eroticism as intimacy increases" affects the interpretation of monogamy for gay male relationships.[49] Probably few within the Judeo-Christian tradition move toward open relationships to this extreme.

Mutual fidelity should not exclude sensual expressions in friendships. Some forms of physical expression are always present in intimate and deep friendships. For example, Heyward, whose work attempts to articulate the nature of just relationships, notes that there can be a category of "erotic friendship" that is not defined by sex but by affection and reaching out to each other in mutual care and love. She suggests that

> learning to value sexual pleasure as a moral good requires that we be faithful to our commitments. This is always an obligation that involves a willingness to work with our sexual partner, or partners, in creating mutual senses of assurance that our relationships are being cared for. Thus we are obligated to be honest—real—with each other and to honor rather than abuse each other's feelings.[50]

Heyward's reflections on intimacy in sexual friendships and the meaning of fidelity are provocative. The basis for her understanding lies in the assumption that friendships between persons who share intimacy will naturally involve physically reaching out to one another and sharing affection. The precise nature of that affection, however, will be determined by the persons involved and by the context of mutuality, love, and justice.

Responsible pastoral caregivers, when working on issues of mutuality and fidelity, will approach women with openness and clarity. Traditional understandings of monogamy should neither be espoused nor ignored. Likewise, openness to significant relationships outside the primary partnership should not be confused with a lack of any boundaries around the covenantal partnership. What is most important for women in lesbian partnerships is for each person to bring clarity to what she expects within the relationship. One of the difficulties for women in lesbian relationships who move toward a more permissive structure for their relationships is that they may neglect to talk clearly about their expectations, which often results in deep hurt and conflict. While women in lesbian partnerships who are involved in nonmonogamous relationships often are open about these relationships,[51] this does not mean that pain is not present.

Pastoral caregivers who expand notions of mutuality and fidelity beyond the realm of sex will be the most helpful. What is critical for partners is mutually coming to terms with a covenant that clearly states the boundaries and expectations for their relationships. The caregiver might help them by asking questions that expand notions of mutuality beyond sexual fidelity: How do they hold one another accountable in the context of their partnership? How will they know when a friendship outside the boundaries of their primary commitments is distracting from their mutual holding of each other? Do they experience the other as holding on too tightly or as being too casual about the boundaries of their partnership? Answering such questions can help women in lesbian partnerships to consider carefully the nature of their covenants with each other.

Seasons in Partnerships

Love, justice, and mutuality provide the moral and ethical guidelines for developing covenants that are vital and healthy for women in lesbian relationships. These qualities can become integral pieces around which women develop partnerships, honoring their commitments to one another, to their faiths, and to the communities in which they are engaged. They are ideals that take shape and form over the lifetime of a partnership.

Covenants, as noted above, are flexible and dynamic. Brueggemann's reminder that families are places where covenants are made, kept, broken, and remade can be extremely helpful for lesbian partnerships. As women know one another over time, they discover new ways of relating that can invite the partnership into deeper levels of love, justice, and mutuality. As is true in other relationships, women who love women move through various cycles, stages, or seasons in their relationships. During the ebb and flow of seasons in partnerships there are many opportunities for women to renegotiate or to end their relationships.

Betty Berzon, a psychotherapist by profession, notes that professional caregivers typically assume that lesbian relationships are not long lasting. Three factors contribute to this way of thinking: the historical perspective that attributes failures in lesbian relationships to their "immorality," the ongoing lack of legal and social support, and the relative invisibility of long-term committed partnerships. Many lesbian relationships, having been formed and maintained in relative secrecy, are not known about or talked about.[52] As a result of these and other factors, women join in partnerships hoping that their relationship will last, but not always trusting deeply that it will. Given this sense of instability, it is not uncommon for partnerships to deteriorate or fade, sometimes prematurely. Other partnerships move through seasons of relating in ways that enrich and deepen their covenants. Caregivers would do well to have a schema for thinking about covenantal partnerships and their unfolding stages.

D. Merilee Clunis and G. Dorsey Green, in a book titled *Lesbian Couples*, have outlined six stages of relationships: prerelationship, romance, conflict, acceptance, commitment, and collaboration.[53] Their model may be useful in pastoral care, but, as in all developmental models, the stages they suggest are more flowing and connected than is evident from their description. Hence, partners may find themselves leaning into a new phase while still dealing with the structures of the previous way of relating. Each partnership moves through the seasons in its own manner, reflecting the individuality of the particular covenant.[54]

In the *prerelationship* stage women make initial choices about getting to know each other based upon emotional, physical, and sexual attractions.

Common anxieties during this getting-to-know-you phase are present as women attempt to negotiate their sexual interactions with one another. As in many relationships, decisions made during this phase may not be guided by intentional and direct conversation and thought. For example, partners may assume things about the meaning of the relationship rather than intentionally talking about these matters of choice. During this season, women in relationships should be encouraged to articulate their needs and wants to each other as clearly as possible.

During the second season, *romance*, "[m]erging and fusion are both the goal and the reality."[55] This is often one of the most exclusive intervals in the relationship as partners enjoy exploring each other emotionally, physically, spiritually, and sexually, to the exclusion of their other friends. During this time, issues of intimacy emerge as women experience the romance of the new relationship. Clunis and Green note that the lack of ritual structures (such as dating, going steady, etc.) encourages women "to view love, sex and marriage, or commitment, as chain-linked."[56] In other words, love, sex, marriage, commitment may blend into one another almost immediately and progressively without adequate time for reflection and negotiation. The temptation to move too quickly during this stage into some kind of formal commitment is present in many relationships. Covenants established at this point in the relationship often need renegotiation later. Partners experience such a strong liaison with each other at this stage that they have not yet discovered their differences. Hints of disagreements may lead them toward the next season.

The third season, *conflict*, is often difficult for women in lesbian partnerships. Again, because women have been socialized not to deal well with conflict or with power, it is difficult for partners to negotiate their way through this stage and into the next. Hence, many lesbian relationships dissolve during this season. Sometimes this is appropriate as women discover that their differences are more than their relationship can handle. Without the social structures or supportive community necessary to move through the conflict, however, there may be a tendency to prematurely end the relationship. Women may seek assistance from pastoral caregivers in the midst of such conflict. The specialist who neither prematurely pushes for an end to the relationship nor treats the conflict superficially can invite women into deeper and more honest levels of communicating. Verifying the importance of conflict as a time to foster love, justice, and mutuality with each other can promote partnerships that are empowering rather than destructive. Women who work through this season can move into the next season with the deeper appreciation and love necessary to move to the next stage.

The fourth season is *acceptance*. Here partners experience "a sense of stability—even of contentment and deep affection."[57] Building upon growth that occurred in the previous stage, women step back from the deep intensity of togetherness and each approaches the other as a person who brings a unique history, including limitations and gifts, into the partnership. Pastoral care specialists can help women recognize that "[t]hey are in a position to change the pattern, and create the kind of partnership they want, based on the here and now."[58]

In the fifth season, *commitment*, relationships take on the steadfastness required for long-term covenantal partnerships. Notions of being separate and together can be particularly helpful during this season as partners discover their needs for aloneness as well as for togetherness. Choices continue to be made about maintaining the partnership; however, there is a greater awareness during this season of how much the covenant has changed since its inception. This knowledge creates both less fear about future changes as well as more grace to deal with the inevitable disappointments and hurts that occur in every relationship. The ongoing need to negotiate about friendships with persons outside the context of the primary partnership may arise during this phase. Here pastoral caregivers and lesbian partners may find themselves discussing monogamy and mutual fidelity in the relationship.[59]

Relationships that are long-lasting, according to Clunis and Green, move toward a sixth phase, *collaboration*, "where the women focus on something bigger than the two of them to share with the world."[60] At times this appears in the form of generativity, as women continue to nurture children who have been a part of the relationship or think about bringing children into the partnership through birth or adoption. Sometimes women find renewed energy to engage in social causes and proactive campaigns for justice. Clunis and Green suggest that this phase of the relationship can also mark a return to other seasons in the relationship as partners continue to confront issues that are long lasting. "However, this renewed relationship has a history of survival and is usually more resilient and stable than it was the first time around."[61]

Covenantal partnerships move through seasons that are significant in developing qualities of relatedness that empower and expand the relationship. Engaging women in reflection upon these dynamics offers the opportunity to partners to intentionally name the pieces of their covenant, to discern where the covenant is not working, to think about how they may wish to change dynamics in the relationship, and to continue to nurture qualities of love, justice, and mutuality.

Pastoral Counseling with Jeanne and Sharon

For the pastoral care specialist, a number of avenues present themselves for working with Jeanne and Sharon. However, given the content of this chapter, it seems appropriate to frame the conversations around Sharon and Jeanne's understandings, interpretations, and experiences of covenant.

They have expressed their connection to the church by approaching a pastoral representative, and it is safe to assume that sensitivity to their commitments of faith should be present in the counseling. Building upon the qualities of love, justice, and mutuality, it is possible to explore with Sharon and Jeanne the nature of their developing covenantal partnership.

Listening carefully to clues about what season the relationship is in will help the counselor clarify the direction to take in conversations with Jeanne and Sharon. For example, they have known each other for almost a year and have not shared a living space during that time. While living apart does not suggest, in and of itself, that the relationship has not endured several seasons, the caregiver should note how notions of romance are talked about in the partnership. Offering Sharon and Jeanne the opportunity to verbalize the kinds of commitments and promises they have made to each other may provide insight. Hearing the story of their months together and pausing with them to acknowledge and celebrate the significant moments along the way that have deepened their partnership signals an affirmation from the pastoral counselor as to the goodness of caring for each other. Paying particular attention to how conflicts have been handled helps the counselor discern whether they have left the stage of romance or are in the season of conflict. Given the brevity of the relationship at this point, it would not be unusual for them to be moving between the romance and conflict seasons. For purposes of this chapter, we will assume this to be the case for Jeanne and Sharon.

A brief look at some of the concerns that may arise with Jeanne and Sharon offers insight into counseling with other lesbian partnerships. These concerns are not indicators of whether Jeanne and Sharon will become lifetime partners, but they may suggest areas to explore as they continue to think about what it means to be involved in a covenantal partnership. Developing meaningful covenants is often complicated by the lack of social structures available to them where they might discuss formally the nature of an ongoing relationship. The gift of a proactive pastoral counselor is to pursue conversations in ways that assist the partners in reflecting upon their covenants by recounting past experiences in the partnership, present areas of concern and celebration, and future hopes and visions.

Since one of the primary qualities of covenantal partnership is love, exploring with Sharon and Jeanne how they experience the love between them can be a way of inviting them to reflect upon the meaning of their relationship. Talking with them about the significance of friendship can evoke a sense of what is at the base of their partnership. For example, in the midst of the flow of conversation, pastoral caregivers want to keep some of these questions in mind: Is this a friendship that is built around deep and genuine care, or does it feel more like one that has been initiated but which has not yet approached a significant depth? Do they give evidence that their love for one another will sustain them through the inevitable conflicts, or have they not yet discovered that aspect of friendship in each other?

Being attentive to issues of sexuality, the second component of love, can offer the pastoral care specialist insight into the meaning of this quality in the partnership. The counselor should not avoid talking about sex; at the same time the counselor should remember that sex is not the only aspect of the partnership that makes their relationship distinctive. It is undoubtedly more helpful to engage partners in thinking about sexuality from a rather broad perspective. Noting how comfortable they are in talking about how they express their love for each other sometimes leads to helpful conversations about internalized feelings of sexuality. For example, if one of the partners has struggled with self-affirmation of sexuality or one is a sexual abuse survivor, sexuality can be an extremely important area for dialogue.

The third aspect of love, having a sense of security in the relationship, may emerge as Sharon and Jeanne talk about how they have handled conflict. For some partners tension in the relationship creates the anxiety or fear that the other will be disappointed or will leave. Helping women learn how to be secure and how to fight fair, particularly if they have not yet survived the season of conflict, is a proactive way of assisting them as they move toward that season of their life together and may keep them from attempting to avoid areas of difference. At the same time, it is important to explore with Jeanne and Sharon how they handle the insecurity of living in a world that does not always feel accepting and affirming.

Finally, in assessing the quality of love in this relationship the caregiver should consider how Jeanne and Sharon interact with their friends, families, colleagues, and others. If Jeanne and Sharon are in the earlier seasons of their partnership, they probably have not yet moved to the place of expanding their friendships while still maintaining primary fidelity with each other. Again, bearing in mind certain questions wil help the pastoral counselor clarify how these partners experience the broader community: Is there a sense of fear or jealousy as they talk about former lovers or friends? Do they depend upon the relationship to fill all their emotional needs at the moment or do they have an extended community that supports them? Do they share all their friends or do they maintain separate friendship systems? Have they experienced a lot of support for their relationship or do only a few people really know about their emerging partnership? How do their families and friends relate to them as a family? Are there persons to whom they turn in times of conflict with each other?

The qualitative presence of justice will probably emerge at various times in the conversations with Sharon and Jeanne. However, special attention should be given to issues of power, the degree of honesty and courage in confrontations they have with each other, and their concern for creating just relationships beyond themselves. For example, since money becomes one of the expressions of power in relationships, it is important to discuss how financial matters are handled in the partnership. There is not one right way for lesbians to deal with money other than that they ought to find ways to share power and access to their resources. Because of the systemic injustice with which lesbian partnerships must deal, practical matters that are often low priorities early in the relationship may need discussion: wills, powers of attorney for medical and fiscal matters, setting up separate or joint savings accounts, and assigning beneficiaries in life insurance policies. This is particularly important in lesbian partnerships because there may be no legal structures that otherwise protect them in certain circumstances. The caregiver should have the name of an attorney who specializes in working with lesbian partnerships to whom partners such as Sharon and Jeanne can be referred if they are interested in exploring these matters as a part of their covenant to share power.

The issues of mutual vulnerability and mutual fidelity may arise with Sharon and Jeanne during discussion of some of the matters mentioned above. Determining whether their trust is built on genuine experiences with each other, or on naive hope, or on assumptions about the other can reveal the depth of mutuality in the relationship. This can be significant because each partner may be in a different place in terms of the amount of trust. Added to this is the very real possibility that issues of mutual fidelity—whether in terms of sexual boundaries for the relationship or of holding each other accountable for particular balances of power in the partnership—have probably not been addressed sufficiently if Sharon and Jeanne are still in the season of romance.

The final issue apparent in the case of Jeanne and Sharon is their desire to have some kind of formal service to mark their commitment to each other. Given whatever is learned in the conversations about love, justice, and mutuality, the pastoral care specialist will be able to work with this partnership on the meaning of such a service. There is a difference between a ritual that celebrates the entry into a process of getting to know each other and one that signifies that the partnership has moved to the season of commitment or collaboration. Assisting Sharon and Jeanne in articulating how they understand the season of their relationship will give them more clarity about what they intend to communicate by having some kind of formal service.

Denominations and the members they represent do not agree about whether covenant services in the context of congregational life are appropriate. Similarly, consensus is lacking within the lesbian community about whether holy unions signal what most partners intend to communicate about their covenants. However, some kind of ritual moment that formally recognizes a particular partnership and its present meaning and future hopes can hold intense meaning for persons like Sharon and Jeanne. Jung and Smith aptly note:

> One problem with developing a new category of religiously blessed unions is that they are isolated from a broader support network. It is not sufficient to affirm a relationship via symbolization and celebration if no attendant or consequential structures are in place to honor and nurture it. It is the equivalent of stepping across the threshold into a vacuum. It is a door to nowhere. In other words, we cannot create ritual *structures* in the same ways that we can create ritual *moments*. Without broader social, economic, and legal support, "blessed unions" are relegated to inferior, secondary, or subordinate status.[62]

The social, economic, and legal supports about which Jung and Smith talk are often visibly absent from covenantal partnerships. Even though a pastoral representative may participate in the ritual moment, usually there is no parallel support system beyond those friends and family members who may gather to share in the covenantal partnership. This, however, does not mean that ritual moments do not have profound meaning.

One final encouragement to pastoral care specialists on this matter: women need to be invited to claim and celebrate as many significant events in their relationship as they can name. One of the gifts of being in lesbian partnerships can be the opportunity to remember the covenant and renew its meaning throughout the year by celebrating various significant moments. There are probably not many persons who think to inquire about the events Sharon and Jeanne understand to be significant, nor why they are important to them. The pastoral counselor who asks and celebrates with them will be one who has affirmed, honored, and renewed with them their covenantal partnership in meaningful ways.

Covenants, as noted earlier in this chapter, have four elements: the oaths or promises, a community, opportunities for periodic renewal, and dynamic qualities. The qualities of love, justice, and mutuality are developed over time as covenants shift with the emergence of new seasons in relationships. Pastoral caregivers who approach women in lesbian relationships with these understandings are being proactive as they encourage women to build their relationships in meaningful and powerful ways.

Chapter Four

Challenges
to Covenantal Partnerships

Not every lesbian partnership embodies the qualities of love, justice, and mutuality that were articulated in chapter 3. But just as proactive pastoral caregivers cannot assume that all lesbian partnerships are built around these qualitative notions of covenant, specialists ought not to prematurely interpret variations in lesbian relationships as pathological or dysfunctional. Energy, courage, and the willingness to move through struggles and chaos rather than to avoid them are required for nurturing and sustaining covenantal partnerships. This is not easy in a world that often actively discourages partnerships from succeeding, or that remains oblivious to the struggles of lesbians to sustain enduring relationships. The challenges with which this chapter deals are not unique to lesbian partnerships, but they can be the most common and overlooked struggles in these relationships.

Case material will be used to examine four issues in the context of lesbian partnerships: addictions, lesbian battering, sexual abuse and trauma, and enmeshed or fused partnerships. These cases serve to illuminate particularities about lesbian partnerships that can then be appropriated for work with other women who love women. The ultimate therapeutic goal in each case is to strengthen the covenantal partnership by attending to the qualities of love, justice, and mutuality.

Each of the four case studies that follow begins with a description of the background of the case and a brief discussion about the particular dynamics these women face as lesbian partners. Then there is illustration of the ways in which pastoral caregivers and their clients are mutually involved in assessing the strengths and liabilities of partnerships. While each specialist brings specific frames to the task of assessment (e.g., family systems, cognitive-behavioral, psychodynamic, etc.), a uniquely pastoral theological perspective can be offered by attending to how love, justice, and mutuality are embodied in the covenantal partnership. Each case reflection concludes with a short summary of some of the goals that may emerge in working through the issues that the partners present to the pastoral care specialist.

Addictions:
Alcohol and Drugs

Peggy and Sherry have known each other for fifteen years. For the past ten years they have shared ownership of a duplex, each claiming a residence in one-half of the house. They spend most of their evenings and nights together in Peggy's section of the house, but they maintain the appearance of separate quarters and "just a good friendship." They have never actually told anyone in their families of origin that they are lovers, but they have been together long enough that their families consider them best friends and don't ask many questions about their relationship. Peggy comes from a family that is extremely conservative theologically. Both of her parents and an older brother and a younger sister live in a neighboring state. Sherry's family seems to be more open, but Sherry is convinced it would hurt her mother too much if she knew the truth about her relationship with Peggy. Over the years, Peggy and Sherry have maintained their connection to the church, although they often experience deep hurt and despair at the church's official statements about lesbian and gay persons. They think that those who know them in their community of faith would probably be affirming and supportive of their relationship, but they have chosen never to openly profess their relationship to others in the church. Sherry and Peggy are leaders in other social justice concerns in their church, and they have found many like-minded persons whom they trust at an intuitive level.

Sherry and Peggy describe themselves as occasional or social drinkers. Over the past several years, however, Sherry has noticed that Peggy has been drinking more often, especially in response to stresses at work, at church, in their extended family, or within their relationship. Occasionally Sherry has voiced her concerns to Peggy, but Peggy has always vehemently denied that she is dependent upon alcohol. Usually after Sherry mentions her concern to Peggy, the drinking stops for a couple of days or a week until the next crisis or stressor arises and Peggy returns to drinking, claiming that it helps her relax and sleep.

Sherry has grown increasingly concerned about Peggy's drinking and decides that she herself needs support, even if Peggy denies she has a problem. Sherry makes an appointment with the pastoral counselor whose office is located in their church. In the initial session Sherry is somewhat elusive about why she has come. She frames the conversation in terms of her "best friend" who, she suspects, is drinking too much. The pastoral counselor, being sensitive and open, helps Sherry think about how to intervene with her friend and then offers her the opportunity to claim more about the relationship by saying, "Peggy seems to be very important to you. Would you like to tell me more about your relationship to her?" Sherry confides that Peggy is more than just a best friend and wonders if the pastoral counselor would see them together. The counselor and Sherry talk about how to invite Peggy into the next session, being clear that while Peggy's abuse of alcohol may be the primary issue in terms of treatment, there are also relational issues that might be addressed in the context of pastoral counseling. Sherry is able to convince Peggy to attend the next session.

The abuse of alcohol or other drugs is not unique for women in lesbian relationships, of course. What is distinctive for lesbians is the degree to which internalized homophobia, guilt, shame, and heterosexism in the church and the culture contribute to their addiction. Most of the research on the incidence of alcoholism in the lesbian community suggests that the rate of alcohol addiction among lesbians may be as much as three times higher than in the heterosexual community.[1] Add to this the incidence of other forms of addiction and the level of chemical dependency within the lesbian community is astounding. This high level of abuse probably occurs not because lesbians are more prone to dysfunction than are non-lesbians but because of the interaction of the pressures of being lesbian in the culture. Compounding the problem of drug and alcohol dependency are other issues linked with addiction in women, such as effects of childhood sexual abuse.

Good intentions, accompanied by misconceptions on the part of the care specialist about the contributing factors for alcoholism among lesbians, can result in the delivery of poor care. One misconception about lesbians who abuse alcohol is that women drink to mask unresolved issues of sexuality. Claiming a lesbian identity does not necessarily indicate that persons drink because they are uncomfortable with their sexuality. In the case of Peggy and Sherry it is not at all clear that this is true. In conversations with the pastoral caregiver they present themselves as being comfortable with their lesbian identity, but unwilling to deal with the potential anger from their families or from their church community if they were to reveal that identity. The lack of self-affirmation and acceptance may intensify the drinking but should not be understood as the cause of the alcoholism.[2]

A second misconception is that the presence of gay bars in the lesbian community is directly responsible for the high incidence of alcoholism. Bars traditionally have been places to socialize and meet one another in the lesbian and gay communities. In the past there were relatively few public arenas for women to meet others who share their orientation, and bars have become important places within the lesbian community. However, the presence of a place to socialize should not be viewed as the single factor responsible for the high rate of addictions among the lesbian community. Peggy and Sherry, for example, do not frequent bars. Their case serves as a reminder to pastoral care specialists not to assume that those who do visit bars are alcoholics, or that women who don't patronize bars can never be addicted.[3]

A third misconception arises from the common stereotype of the alcoholic as male. Many people in our culture do not think about women as abusers of alcohol or drugs. Pastoral counselors or other caring professionals who assume that women do not drink as much as men, or assume that women are less likely than men to become alcoholics, can collude with the alcoholism by not confronting it or by failing to ask about the presence and use of alcohol. For women like Peggy and Sherry who do not reveal their lesbian partnership, alcoholism is just one more secret. The invisibility of being women alcoholics connects with the invisibility of being lesbian.[4]

Counselors should be aware of three significant factors when working with lesbians on issues of addiction. First, treatment or recovery programs can be extremely important in the process of recovery. However, for those who are closeted, such as Sherry and Peggy, entering a treatment center or recovery program often results in having to be honest with family members who may not have previously been aware of their sexual orientation. The work for the family is intensified as they struggle to understand the alcoholism while also attempting to deal with what it means that their relative is in a lesbian partnership.[5]

Second, it is normal that sex will arise as an issue for lesbian partnerships where one woman is addicted. The patterns and ways of relating to each other, combined with the numbing effects of the alcohol or drugs, may cause low sexual satisfaction within the partnership. In the process of recovery there may be tremendous change in this area. JoAnn Loulan, one of the most prolific writers about the sexual lives of lesbians, notes that "[n]inety-five percent of [her] sample reported changes in their sexual functioning as a result of sobriety."[6] In the early stages of recovery the satisfaction level of sex in partnerships usually decreases. She notes that for some women their recovery marks one of the few times they have engaged in sexual experiences without being under the influence of alcohol or drugs. As sobriety becomes a way of life, those in Loulan's study noted improvement in their sexual lives. Others note that those who have been compulsive about alcohol sometimes turn to compulsive sexual behavior in the early stages of sobriety, thus affecting the partnership in a different manner.[7]

Finally, pastoral care specialists should be aware that women's relationships often deteriorate and do not survive the first stages of recovery.[8] The intensity of changing and renegotiating earlier ways of relating requires more work than many partnerships can endure. Recognizing the detrimental effects of addiction on the partnership demands courage if women are to shift the grounds of their covenant. The external support network of families and friends needed for such changes in partnerships is not always present. Given these realities, it is understandable why many women struggle with alcohol or other addictions but find few internal or external resources that are helpful in their struggles.

The initial process of assessment with Peggy and Sherry should include an evaluation for alcoholism. If the pastoral care specialist is not trained in such endeavors, Sherry and Peggy should be referred to someone who is trained in alcohol and drug use assessment and in recovery—preferably someone in the local community or the surrounding area who works well with lesbians and chemical dependency. The pastoral counselor who takes the trouble to explore these resources on behalf of lesbian partners will provide invaluable assistance as well as make prophetic statements about the importance of providing the best care possible to lesbian partners.

In the context of work with Peggy and Sherry, it is appropriate for the counselor to have them work on the assessment as a joint task, inviting each to respond to questions about the way alcohol has affected their relationship. The evaluation and intervention for alcoholism, however, must be done before other issues in the partnership can be assessed. Patricia Huffman identifies three components in assessing the nature of alcohol abuse: evaluating the level of denial, weighing the effect alcohol has on other aspects of their individual and corporate lives, and creating a recovery program to meet special needs.[9]

Finally, after the assessment of alcoholism and development of an individual recovery plan with Peggy, the pastoral care specialist can then work with Sherry and Peggy on reshaping a covenant that is changing and dynamic. Inquiring about the history of their partnership can reveal the nature of the present covenant and the seasons through which this relationship has evolved. Sherry's revelation that in the past she has confronted Peggy about her drinking suggests that there has been conflict earlier in their relationship. Since their story and outward appearances seem to point toward a sense of security in their relationship, the counselor could assume that they are at least in the season of acceptance, if not commitment or collaboration. The maturity that they have experienced in moving through earlier conflicts in their fifteen-year relationship sets the groundwork for how they now renegotiate the covenant by which they want to live. Attending to the qualities of love as expressed in conversations about their relationship provides an opportunity for Sherry and Peggy to affirm the positive aspects of their covenant.

This case raises concerns for justice in a unique way because Sherry and Peggy have been involved in their local church in promoting justice issues. Helping them articulate how their commitments to justice for others intersects with the development of honesty, openness, courage, and fortitude in their own relationship offers an occasion for them to examine how they relate with each other. In a parallel manner, working with Sherry and Peggy will raise issues of how justice might be extended to them by others whom they have come to respect in their church. Bringing a pastoral theological perspective can provide new opportunities for them to connect the injustices they experience in their life with the commitments of their church.

The pastoral care specialist talks with Peggy and Sherry about how they have held each other's best interest at heart to assess mutuality. In some ways Sherry has taken responsibility for Peggy's drinking by approaching the pastoral caregiver. At the same time, she now has the opportunity to hold Peggy accountable for the effect the drinking has had on their relationship. Enabling Sherry and Peggy to talk about how they mutually care for and nurture each other in the partnership can assist them in talking about how they also might hold each other accountable. The counselor should be attentive to whether one partner is more giving and nurturing than the other.[10] A challenge to the balance of their relationship will require effort from both as they struggle to find mutual ways to relate.

In this case, as in some of the cases that follow, the pastoral care specialist needs to be clear about the difference between work with an individual and work with a partnership. Peggy must work on her recovery issues, and Sherry must work on issues that surface in her individual life. However, without getting in the way of those individual efforts, a pastoral counselor might also work with Sherry and Peggy together on supporting their covenantal partnership.

The following goals may emerge as pastoral caregivers attempt to strengthen the covenantal qualities of love, justice, and mutuality in partnerships:

1. *Working with Peggy and Sherry as they come out to parents and staff in treatment centers or recovery programs.* Before any other kind of work can be done in the partnership, the alcoholism must be confronted. Few treatment centers offer services to lesbian clients specifically designed for their needs. Hence, proactive pastoral counselors will need to be sensitive to what it means for Peggy to enter a program either on an in-patient or on an out-patient basis. Questions about revealing the partnership to others will undoubtedly emerge. For example, neither Peggy's family nor Sherry's family has been told of the partnership. A pastoral counselor can be immensely helpful in thinking through with Sherry and Peggy about what they want to say to those in the treatment center or to their families. Finding ways to educate and work with the families and

the treatment center in a direct but careful manner can assist Peggy and Sherry in their own recovery. They will have more time to focus on their issues rather than on having to educate those in the treatment program about what it means to be lesbian.

2. *Connecting spirituality and sexuality.* One of the gifts of the pastoral counselor, in particular, may be helping Peggy and Sherry connect their faith and spiritual commitments to their lives as lesbian partners in the process of recovery. Since many treatment programs focus on issues of spirituality, this can be an opportunity for conversations with Peggy and Sherry about what it means to be blessed with the gift of sexuality. Robert J. Kus, who has worked extensively in addiction and recovery for lesbians and gay men, suggests that the first step of AA (admitting one is powerless over alcohol) can be helpful as they think about their sexuality. Kus suggests that those who understand themselves to be born lesbian can claim a powerlessness to choose their sexual orientation. This, in turn, can provide freedom for some people and raise their internal sense of self-worth.[11]

3. *Creating justice in their partnership and their communities.* The pastoral counselor who can help Peggy and Sherry frame the issues of their relationship in terms of justice will be helpful in shifting the dynamics of their relationship toward new patterns. Expanding their awareness that they are oppressed persons who live their lives in the midst of injustices perpetrated against them can be significant for Peggy and Sherry. Helping them articulate this in the context of their commitments of faith can assist them in relating to their families and their church. As they work to be more honest with themselves and others about the nature of their covenant, it is possible that others may, in turn, be invited to work for justice on behalf of lesbians and gay men.

4. *Expanding their community.* Channeling Peggy and Sherry into twelve-step groups designed primarily for lesbians can be beneficial. Many larger cities now have such groups. The power of these groups is that women do not have to fear that their lifestyle will be an issue for someone in the group, nor do they have to monitor things that they say for fear of revealing too much about their orientation.

> There is a greater openness and freedom to talk about themselves, their partners, and their recovery programs. Choosing a sponsor who is lesbian can help lesbians move through the process more quickly since the sponsor also has a sense of how difficult it is to be a lesbian in recovery.[12]

Peggy and Sherry bring to the pastoral care specialist the strength of a covenant that has assisted them through the seasons of their common life. The gift of the pastoral counselor in this case is to affirm and strengthen the covenantal partnership by providing a space for Sherry and Peggy to create visions for what it might mean to be partners into the future.

Lesbian Battering

Jane and Phyllis have been involved with each other for the past eleven years. About nine years ago they had a "holy union" service, celebrated by a friend who was a pastor at an open and affirming church. They have not been involved in the church but have a clear understanding that they are partnered for life. In their mid-forties, they are middle-class lesbians who have established themselves as leaders within the women's community. Jane is more politically active, speaking often at lesbian and gay political events. Because of their work lives they are established and well-respected in professional organizations within the community. Phyllis and Jane have been publicly open about their lives and their commitments since the formation of their partnership. From the outside it would appear that they are the success story for covenantal partnerships between women.

However, what few people have witnessed over the years are the incredible fights Jane and Phyllis have. They often engage in verbal combat, with Jane demeaning Phyllis or accusing her of being unfaithful in the partnership. Sometimes the fights become physical; Jane is the more controlling of the two and the one with more physical strength. Very rarely does Jane hit Phyllis anywhere on her body that can be seen by others. Usually the bruises are covered by clothing because they are on Phyllis's upper arms, stomach, or upper legs. Over the years Phyllis has become accustomed to leaving their home after the physical violence occurs, checking into a motel for one or two nights. Jane is always remorseful the next day, sending flowers to Phyllis at work and promising she will never hit her again. Jane has agreed a couple of times to see a counselor, but she claims she can't find one who is good at working with lesbians and one whom she can trust not to disclose her battering to others. Internally, she carries great fear about being exposed and does not want those within the lesbian community to see this side of her. Phyllis knows that Jane grew up in a household where physical fighting between mother and father was an ordinary occurrence. Understanding this, Phyllis has remained committed to Jane and trusts that Jane wants to stop the physical violence.

An additional problem is that Jane controls the financial arrangements for their partnership and keeps track of their investments. Jane makes almost twice as much money as Phyllis, they jointly own property and vehicles, and they have assigned each other as beneficiaries on wills and power of attorney forms. Phyllis feels that there is too much at stake in this partnership to think about ending it because of the violence.

Recently Jane and Phyllis were doing some repairs on their house when Jane got angry about something Phyllis did. Jane picked up a large board and hit Phyllis in the ribs. Phyllis was in extreme pain but drove herself to the hospital. When asked, she told the nurse that she had slipped on the steps. Suspecting that she was not telling the truth and that she had been hit by someone, the nurse confronted Phyllis and offered her a referral to the chaplain on call. Because Phyllis was extremely vulnerable, tired, angry, and hurt, she was willing to talk. Phyllis confided in the chaplain that she was in a lesbian partnership and agreed to ongoing conversation.

The most common misconception in working with lesbian partnerships is that women do not hit other women and that battering is not present in the lesbian community. The truth is that lesbian relationships are not immune from domestic violence as it is defined here: "any pattern of behavior designed to coerce, dominate, or isolate within a relationship or the exercise of any form of power to maintain control. Abuse is always based on unequal power."[13] Physical violence between women does exist, and reckoning with this reality is imperative so as not to minimize abuse when it does occur.[14]

The form of such abuse is as diverse as it is in other relationships. For example, there may be sexual abuse within the partnership, destruction of a partner's property, or economic restrictions placed within the relationship to maintain control by the abuser. An added weapon in the violence perpetrated by women against women is the threat to expose another woman's sexual orientation. While this does not seem to be the case with Phyllis and Jane because of their openness in the community, for some partners intimidation can occur when one person's secrecy about orientation becomes a powerful means of control and abuse by the other.

There are many reasons why women physically abuse one another. Most of the causes of battering by men are also operative for lesbians, such as the need to maintain control and power within a relationship, or as a form of learned behavior passed on from families of origin. However, there are two realities that make lesbian battering distinct from what happens in traditional heterosexual relationships. First, as noted in the previous chapter, there is an intensity about women's partnerships and friendships that results in strong emotional ties. Given this dynamic, there may be less inclination for the partner to remove herself from a relationship when violence occurs. The desire for closeness with other women may also cause lesbians to move back into partnerships too quickly after an abusive episode. Added to this is the complexity of living in secret relationships where persons maintain silence about what is significant in their lives or, if they are open in the community as in the case of Phyllis and Jane, there may be tremendous pressure from other lesbians to maintain the relationship and to deny that the abuse exists.

A second reality for women in lesbian relationships is pointed out by Rochelle Klinger, who notes that

> [s]exism can also be operative in lesbian relationships, particularly when one or both partners adopt male/female roles. Just as homophobia can be internalized by gays and lesbians, a lesbian can batter her partner, partly because she has internalized negative attitudes toward women.[15]

Women who love women struggle with internal images of themselves and one another that reflect women as victims or as unhealthy persons. Women in lesbian relationships sometimes take out their internal negative feelings upon the women they love. While this is not an excuse for the battering, it is a factor in the violence that occurs in some relationships. This acting out of negative images is particularly present in relationships that involve more rigid understandings of male/female roles, with one person in the partnership taking on traditionally male qualities while the other accepts the traditionally female role. Again, this does not seem to be the case with Phyllis and Jane, although they have opted for a pattern in which one woman controls the relationship more than the other in terms of leadership and in the regulation of financial resources.

Turning to assessment, there are three issues to consider in this case. First, the assessment begins with each individual in the situation, rather than with the partners. In other words, the initial focus should be on each of the women individually in therapy rather than on issues of mutual partnership. A common mistake is made by well-intentioned pastoral counselors who, wanting to assist the partners in maintaining their relationship, minimize the abuse and agree to see women together without first assessing the extent of the abuse. Based on the false assumption that women do not mean to hurt one another, or that women can't really hurt one another too badly, this intervention creates two difficulties. First, it does not offer Phyllis the freedom she needs to voice her experience of the abuse without fear that what she says may create more anger and violence in Jane. The current theory on domestic violence suggests that appropriate care means treating women separately before negotiating joint therapy. Violence often escalates during counseling done on a partnership basis. Second, working with Phyllis and Jane together does not offer an intentional place to confront Jane with her perpetration of the violence. One of the first goals in working with Jane and Phyllis is to refer them to separate counselors who specialize in the treatment of batterers and victims/survivors. Any work to be done cooperatively can be done only when each has individually assessed her participation in the relationship.

Individual assessment also allows each woman to identify her needs and desires for the partnership. It is not clear that Jane and Phyllis ought to stay together permanently, nor is it clear that they need to end their partnership. What is clear is that the violence does not provide a safe environment in which they can work on a covenant of love, justice, and mutuality. A temporary separation sometimes assists partners to articulate individual needs in the partnership. Suspending judgments about the viability of the relationship for the future assists both Phyllis and Jane as they explore their individual lives in relation to the partnership.

Second, issues of power and dominance should be assessed in working with Jane and Phyllis. Confronting the powerfulness of one partner and the seeming lack of power of the other can assist Phyllis and Jane in thinking about what it means for them to share power and to work toward justice in relating to each other and to others. This is an issue not only for the partnership but for other relationships they have with friends, colleagues, or extended family. Again, this assessment is best done individually as each works on how she has come to understand her primary way of functioning in the partnership.

There is potential in this partnership to work toward more mutuality. However, at the moment the issues of violence are creating such chaos in their patterns of relating that mutuality is a difficult and arduous task to be accomplished only after much intense work. For example, open and honest communication will ultimately mean that Phyllis has to articulate her needs more clearly and that Jane has to learn other ways of dealing with conflict. With extraordinary work Phyllis and Jane may eventually build a partnership that demonstrates mutuality and just relating rather than abuse and dominance.

The goals in working with women like Phyllis and Jane will vary with each individual. The pastoral care specialist should neither dismiss altogether the importance of the partnership to Phyllis or Jane, nor encourage the women to move back together too quickly. The individual goals that follow are significant to address before any kind of conversation about joint counseling can occur.

For Phyllis, goals include:

1. *Working with Phyllis on issues of safety.* A primary objective in working with Phyllis is to help her think about her own safety. Normally referral to a shelter is helpful for bat-

tered women, but not every shelter accepts women from lesbian relationships. At the moment the relational covenant she has with Jane has been violated by the physical violence and a new covenant must be established. Before developing any new covenant Phyllis needs to plan for her safety. Helping Phyllis frame the issue of safety from the perspective of making a covenant of love for herself can assist her in knowing that meeting individual needs in partnership is not contradictory to meaningful and right relationships with others. A new covenant with Jane cannot be established until Phyllis is safe and secure in her love for herself.

2. *Allowing Phyllis to reflect upon power in relationship.* One problem for Phyllis is that she assumes that love of Jane is more important than love of self, ultimately giving power in the relationship over to Jane. Her socialization process probably included, as it has for most women, a focus on being the caretaker of others. Seeking ways to embrace her love of self can be important if she is to connect with her own needs and desires in relationships. Increasing in Phyllis the desire to exercise her power in ways that create more just relationships where power is shared can encourage her to think about her partnership with Jane from a new perspective.

3. *Encouraging Phyllis to connect with other women who have been victimized.* A part of Phyllis's self-discovery and healing can and should take place in the context of hearing other women tell their stories. Referring Phyllis to a battered women's support group can allow her the grace to share her pain with others. Again, this may be extremely difficult in some communities because of the lack of support for lesbian relationships. Phyllis must also refuse to carry the awesome responsibility of having the perfect lesbian partnership. Being open and honest in a group of other victims/survivors can assist her in not carrying this mantle for the community. A pastoral caregiver should encourage Phyllis to listen to the stories of others in the midst of their survival and recovery so that she may gain the strength she needs to seek a relationship of love, justice, and mutuality.

For Jane the goals are somewhat different, yet they reflect an awareness of the partnership in some of the same ways as did Phyllis's goals:

1. *Confronting Jane with her behavior.* This may be, perhaps, one of the most difficult goals in working with Jane and Phyllis. There may be too much at stake for Jane to be honest about her behavior. Depending on the structure of her defenses and her ability to be honest with herself and others, Jane may be unwilling to work on her issues of battering. She may not feel enough internal security to trust either herself or others with her story.

2. *Encouraging Jane to talk with other women who batter or attend a batterer's group.* Finding a lesbian batterer's group is extremely difficult in most communities. In some larger cities this area is being addressed, but finding groups specifically designed for women who abuse other women is almost impossible. It is also unlikely that Jane will feel comfortable in a typical batterer's group, which usually consists of straight men. What is essential, however, is that the pastoral care specialist work with Jane in whatever way possible to broaden her support network and encourage more honest and open communication with selected others. Confessing her participation in a relationship where she was the batterer will be extremely difficult, given her role in the lesbian and professional communities. However, finding at least a few persons with whom she can share that piece of her life may invite her to move beyond the denial of the abuse into some kind of honest wrestling with it. Becoming more open and honest may encourage Jane to move toward more just relationships not only with Phyllis but also with others.

3. *Focusing on ways in which Jane can experience mutual vulnerability.* Again, this is probably a difficult issue for Jane. It would seem that Jane and Phyllis have not experienced mutuality in much of their relationship and that Jane, in particular, is not good at being mutually vulnerable with others. Experiencing a therapy group with other women (not necessarily restricted to women batterers) who struggle with issues of control can encourage Jane to be more open and flexible in her relationships.

Only after considerable individual work can pastoral care specialists consider bringing the partners together in therapy. When there is a ground for coming together, the goals for working with Jane and Phyllis become those of fashioning a new covenant that reflects the qualities of love, justice, and mutuality. It might then be possible for them to voice their individual needs and desires in new ways. The process of reshaping a covenant that can assist them in living into the future remains a formidable task in this situation.

Sexual Abuse Survivors

Jerri and Barb have known each other for nine months. Their relationship developed out of their mutual participation in a women's potluck group. Jerri and Barb come from different socioeconomic backgrounds as well as from different cultures. Barb works as an executive secretary and Jerri manages a fast-food restaurant. Barb is twenty-five and has been involved in several short-term relationships and one longer-term relationship that lasted about two years. She has always known she was a lesbian and has been involved only with other women. Jerri is twenty-three and has never been involved in any significant long-term relationship with a male or female. She has spent most of her energy for the past several years trying to advance into upper management at work. She is currently enrolled part-time in business courses and works evenings and weekends. They spend little quality time together but manage to meet for lunch almost daily.

During the course of getting to know each other they have been very cautious about their relationship, particularly in their expressions of sexual intimacy. They have not spent many nights together, and when they have done so, they seemed content just holding each other. Their sexual affection has been limited to kissing and gentle touching or mutual stroking. Recently Barb has been assertive about wanting to be more intimate sexually. But whenever the possibility for more sexual activity emerges, Jerri tends to back away and withdraw emotionally. Barb has responded with care and caution but has become increasingly frustrated by the conflict between Jerri's verbal messages that communicate closeness and her physical messages that convey distance.

Finally, Barb confesses to Jerri that she is not getting what she needs out of the relationship and indirectly confronts Jerri with her pattern of emotional closeness and physical distancing. After much encouragement to talk about what is going on, Jerri confides in Barb that she was once involved in a heterosexual relationship that became abusive. She explained that during junior high she had a crush on one of the male counselors at her camp. They would sneak out of their cabins and walk alone at night along the lake. The night before she was to leave for home, he forced her into having sex. She has never talked with anyone about this, but whenever she feels sexually aroused she becomes fearful and aware of other kinds of emotions such as feeling dirty, unclean, and ashamed. When prior relationships have gotten too intimate or sexual she has backed away. Now, however, she finds herself extremely attracted to Barb and doesn't want the relationship to end because she cannot engage in a fulfilling sexual life. After hearing the story, Barb responds to the depth of pain she experiences in Jerri and suggests that maybe they ought to see a counselor.

Given the fact that a large percentage of women have experienced sexual abuse in some form or another, when two women come together to form a significant partnership they have twice the chance that one of the partners has experienced abuse as does a heterosexual couple.[16] Thus, issues arising from a history of sexual abuse affect many lesbian partnerships. For some the abuse has been extensive, while for others, like Jerri, the abuse occurred in a one-time incident. Whatever the extent of the abuse, it undoubtedly leaves its mark on the victims/survivors and, in turn, on their primary relationships.

While a wealth of literature deals with recovery from sexual abuse, there is considerably less that speaks directly to the partners of lesbians who are in the midst of healing.[17] For some, the theory that lesbians are women who turn to other women rather than to men for sexual intimacy because they have been sexually abused still holds power. This, however, is a misconception about the etiology of homosexuality in women. Sexual abuse does not lead to lesbian identification; a history of being sexually victimized does, however, have a direct impact on the structure of relationships. As in all relationships, persons bring the pain of previous experiences, sometimes in very raw and vulnerable ways, into the context of present relationships. Sexual abuse is distinct in lesbian relationships not because of its presence, but because of the struggle to maintain healthy sexual lives in partnerships that are understood by some to be suspect, at best.

Jerri appears to have feelings that are normal in women who have experienced sexual abuse. Being confused about her own sexual feelings or about those expressed by others, making choices about how to participate in sexual activity without being hurt, having flashback-type experiences during sexual activity, and struggles with discerning the level of comfortable sexual intimacy in new relationships are common experiences for survivors of sexual abuse. Added to this is the complexity of being lesbian. Women who love women have been socialized not only to think negatively of their sexual lives, but to be self-critical about lesbian relationships. Hence, the feelings of discomfort, shame, or fear may be particularly intense for women who love other women.

As in the other cases presented in this chapter, separating the individual issues from those of the partnership is an important step. Probably Jerri will need to do some counseling and special caretaking for herself as she moves into the process of healing and recovery. However, since Barb and

Jerri have approached the pastoral care specialist together, it is appropriate to consider with them what it means to love someone through the healing process from sexual abuse. Referring Jerri to someone for individual work does not necessarily mean a pastoral caregiver has to abandon the partnership. Caregivers should be careful and appropriate in support of Jerri's healing while also attending to the dynamics of the relationship. Pastoral caregivers who can provide a place for partners to deal with some of the tensions and struggles that emerge in the process of healing from sexual abuse can potentially encourage a strong and intentional building of a covenantal relationship.

In terms of assessment, one of the first things to pursue is a consideration of the nature of the covenant between Barb and Jerri. Since they are in the earliest stages of their relationship, they probably have not yet weathered many storms. Their arrival in a pastoral care office can be an opportunity to reflect with them about how they have come to understand their relationship, asking about the promises they have made to each other at this stage of their life. Jerri and Barb appear to be in the romance stage of their partnership. Proactively talking with both of them about what the recovery process is like will help them determine whether they have the commitment to follow the process through with each other. Again, it is best not to judge whether or not a relationship is going to make it through a particular phase in life. Instead, what is needed is the counselor's constant presence to enable the partners to negotiate the struggles and decisions that lie ahead of them.

A related need is for honest and open conversation about how each woman understands love in the context of this new relationship. Testing for the presence of romantic love engages Jerri and Barb in thinking about how they might handle conflicts as they arise. A mature sense of love can empower them to withstand conflict and the dynamics of insecurity that might emerge in the recovery process. Early in the healing process it may be difficult for Barb and Jerri to do anything more than care for one another. Barb may feel left out as Jerri engages in her own healing, or Jerri may feel coerced into sharing more of her process with Barb than she intends. As time goes on, conflicts will present themselves. Assessing Barb and Jerri's ability to have open and honest conversations encourages them to find ways to relate in which Jerri does not feel obligated to share more than she wants and Barb does not feel left out of the process.

Another aspect of assessment should center on the nature of the mutuality that Jerri and Barb seem to experience in each other. Some form of love and care is evident, as it appears to have sustained the relationship thus far, as well as having encouraged Barb and Jerri to seek help together. What is less evident, however, is whether this relationship is built around mutuality. There are many ways to test for mutuality in working with persons healing from sexual abuse, such as an open discussion about what it feels like for Jerri to be the more vulnerable person in the relationship when sexual issues are concerned. In turn, talking about Barb's caretaking role can offer some insight into the presence, or absence, of mutuality. Does Barb see her ability to give more emotionally as a normative way of being in relationship or as a sign of a particular season in their partnership? In similar ways, does Barb always see herself as caregiver in relationships or does Jerri always view herself as the one who has needs in relationships? These questions can ultimately help Jerri and Barb assess what it means for them to be in a mutual relationship where each brings particular needs, histories, vulnerabilities, and gifts.

The goals for working with Jerri and Barb, then, are:

1. *Modeling a safe environment.* Given the history of victimization related to sexual abuse, it is imperative for the pastoral caregiver to provide a safe environment for them to talk about their covenants, their dreams for the future, as well as the realities of the pain through which they must travel. Through open and honest conversation about their feelings about sexual intimacy in their relationship, Barb and Jerri can explore what it means to communicate with tenderness and care. Working with them to articulate what is good about their sexual relationship as well as what feels threatening or fearful offers them an opportunity to explore what it means to be sexual beings who seek intimacy and communion with each other. Modeling safe and nonintrusive communication about sex and sexual feelings can be important.[18] Safety in the context of the pastoral counseling office can help them envision a covenant guided by mutuality, justice, and love.

2. *Reflecting on the seasons of relationships.* It may be beneficial for Barb and Jerri to have a framework for thinking about their relationship together. Since the relationship is relatively new and young, they need to be aware of the struggles and changing dynamics that will occur as they move through the healing process together. If they choose to continue as partners, they will need the assistance and support of persons around them who can remind them about the changes that must happen for women recovering from sexual abuse. Encouraging them to move slowly in building their partnership and to remain honest in their communication with each other can provide a model for negotiating future changes in the relationship.

3. *Encouraging honesty about individual needs.* It may be difficult for Jerri to assert her individual needs in the context of her relationship with Barb. In a parallel manner, it would not be unusual for Barb to expect more closeness or intimacy than Jerri has to offer. Reframing Jerri's withdrawal as a sign of recovery rather than rejection can be helpful, as Barb learns to let go in the relationship and to trust Jerri in the process of her recovery. Loulan suggests that one strategy that can be important in working with partners such as Jerri and Barb is to be aware of the tendency for persons like Barb to deny any painful history she might have.[19] The pastoral care specialist who can assist both of them in being honest with themselves and each other about their needs will invite mutuality into the partnership in new ways.

4. *Inviting Barb and Jerri to stay connected to others.* Given the amount of energy that new relationships can consume, along with the complexity of healing from any kind of sexual abuse, Jerri and Barb might be tempted to begin to isolate or not to expend the energy to connect with others. For Jerri it might be possible to join a women's support group for survivors of sexual abuse or a lesbian support group. Together they might explore ways to connect with others in the community for fun and relaxation. Staying too close in the relationship and isolating from others can create additional tension in the primary relationship since it puts too much focus and attention on the survivor and her recovery.[20] Healing is hard work, and it is important to nurture the romance and the playful sides of relationships while also acknowledging the pain and work involved in recovery.

Focusing with Jerri and Barb on the qualities they would like to have in their relationship and on the dynamic nature of changing covenants can be helpful. They do not need someone who wants to push them into or out of relationship; rather, they need a pastoral care specialist who wants to honor their partnership as they move through the processes ahead of them.

Fusion in Partnerships

Jenny and Nancy are in their mid to late fifties and have been in relationship with each other for six years. During the early years in their relationship they experienced much conflict. At that point most of the tension centered on clarifying expectations each had for the other and resolving some friction between Jenny and one of Nancy's adult children who was still living with Nancy at that time. Jenny has been involved in other significant partnerships, the last one ending about two years before she met Nancy. This is Nancy's second experience in relationship with another woman; the first one occurred while she was still married to her husband. Recognizing that she could not live in two different relationships, she chose to divorce her husband about seven years ago.

Nancy has not been open with any of her three adult children or with her former husband about the reasons for the divorce, but it has given her the freedom she needed to explore her life as a lesbian. The relationship between Nancy and her first lover dissolved shortly after Nancy's decision to divorce. Since then Nancy has spent time exploring her motivations, her life, and her patterns for developing partnerships. Her relationship with Jenny developed slowly, both of them having experienced deep hurt in past intimate relationships. They seem to have negotiated through most of the conflictual season and are now in a period of claiming the goodness of their relationship with greater depth. As a result of these and other dynamics, Nancy and Jenny are very intentional about the way they structure their partnership. They understand their covenant to be one of monogamous partnership and are feeling increasingly more comfortable with their relationship and its potential for enduring in the long term.

Jenny and Nancy have remained fairly closeted, for fear that Nancy would lose her high school teaching job. Jenny holds a job with a company that she knows would not be supportive of her partnership with Nancy, and she prefers to keep her private life separate from her work life. During their six years together they have maintained separate living quarters, but Jenny is rarely at her apartment and spends most of her time at Nancy's. They have made few friends in the lesbian community, and Nancy often states that she feels uncomfortable when they are at women's social events. Jenny and Nancy appear content to spend their free time, weekends, and vacations together.

A crisis developed when Jenny fell ill and was diagnosed with cancer. After undergoing surgery she was put on a regimen of radiation therapy with a good prognosis. It was during this crisis that they discovered they did not have strong friendship systems apart from each other. When Nancy wanted someone to sit with her in the hospital, she couldn't think of anyone to call other than her adult children, who lived elsewhere and who were unaware of the depth of her relationship with Jenny. She began to feel lonely and depressed. Underneath these feelings was what she thought to be an irrational fear that Jenny might die. Nancy began to panic about her life and accepted an invitation from the hospital chaplain to talk. What became evident in the conversation with the chaplain was that Nancy was afraid she would be abandoned by Jenny, either physically or emotionally.

Having spent the past six years working on developing their relationship, they have come to know each other well. They depend upon each other to meet most of their social and emotional needs.

This case reflects a somewhat different type of dilemma from those in the cases previously discussed in this chapter. Lesbian battering, alcoholism, and traumatic sexual abuse are issues that impinge upon the relationship, causing partners to reevaluate and renegotiate ways of relating to one another. The current case, however, lifts up an issue that is internal to the relationship and is a relatively common dilemma for lesbian partners. The closeness women have in relating to each other is sometimes viewed negatively by therapists who work with lesbian partners. This case illuminates the question: Given the intensity of closeness for women in lesbian relationships, when is it legitimate to wonder if a partnership has become fused?

For many family therapists this case immediately signals an enmeshed or fused relationship where there is a lack of clarity about individual and self boundaries. As such, Jenny and Nancy present an issue that is often misdiagnosed or interpreted as pathological, or at the very least as dysfunctional, in the context of lesbian partnerships. From Murray Bowen's work in family systems, the term *fusion* has come to represent "the lower end of a continuum measuring the individual human being's capacity to act and feel as an independent self."[21] In other words, in partnerships where fusion occurs, one partner appears lost in the other's presence (or absence) and seems to deny her own needs and wishes. Women whose relationships represent fusion or enmeshment are those for whom maintaining the relationship becomes so important that individual development or differentiation cannot occur. However, the concept of fusion as utilized in many traditional family therapy strategies is challenged by feminist therapists and, in particular, by persons working with lesbian partnerships. The concern is that the positive aspects of women's relationships are denied by an overemphasis on differentiation.

Before diagnosing the presence of fusion between Nancy and Jenny the pastoral care specialist should assess three factors that impact the development of lesbian partnerships. What often appears as fusion can be understood through the influence of the intrapsychic, interpersonal, and communal spheres on the creation of lesbian partnerships. In noting these spheres of influence on women's relationships, pastoral caregivers should remember that while most lesbians find strong support in the community of women who love women, there are women who focus almost exclusively on their partners. The key is to discern what might be normative, helpful, and healthy for women in partnerships, even when that differs from traditional heterosexual understandings of differentiation.

From an intrapsychic perspective, this case illustrates the ideas presented in the preceding chapters on the development of lesbian identity and covenantal partnerships. Building upon feminist object relations theory, along with the developmental work of persons like Carol Gilligan, it is increasingly clear that women tend to build their worlds around their sense of relatedness rather than around their understanding of individuation. This does not mean that women do not have individual identities; rather, what is intended in this statement is the reminder that

> [t]he goal of development is the increasing ability to build and to enlarge mutually enhancing relationships. The pathway toward this goal involves ... *relational differentiation*, a process of differentiation ... in which the individual articulates increasing levels of complexity, fluidity, choice, and satisfaction in her constellation of relationships.[22]

Part of what this suggests for women in relationship with other women is that it is normal for the structure of a partnership to focus on maintaining ties with the other person in the relationship.

In the interpersonal sphere, women who relate to women at an emotional, physical, sexual, and spiritual level create unique places of intimacy. Lesbian partnerships usually have a strong emphasis on togetherness and sameness, rather than on difference and detachment. A naive reading of the first chapters in this book would suggest that lesbian partners build all of their relationships around mutual goals, understandings, values, and a high level of intimacy. It is true that, for a variety of reasons, women's relationships are often more intense and, as a result, women struggle with negotiating issues of conflict, power, and distance.[23] This should not be interpreted as meaning that all women have only a desire to merge with another and do not understand themselves to be individuals. What is true is that at the interpersonal level women who love women often have a difficult time in negotiating and shaping the balance of intimacy and distance within their partnerships.

From the communal perspective, caregivers must remember that lesbian partnerships often face overt hostility or covert tolerance about their relationships. As a way of protecting themselves and the ones they love, women in partnerships come to depend more on each other than on anyone else. The consequence of this self-protection is a greater focus on the partnership, sometimes in ways that are not ultimately helpful to either the relationship or the individuals in the partnership. As Jo-Ann Krestan and Claudia Bepko note, "fusion issues within relationships may result in part from attempts by the couple to maintain the subsystem within a larger system whose feedback about their relationship would constantly suggest that they dissolve it."[24] Hence, the bonds that women in lesbian partnerships establish may look more intense and fused than those found in traditional heterosexual relationships because the partners have come to rely upon each other in ways that are important to their internal security.

Feminists and those who work closely with women in lesbian partnerships have challenged traditional assumptions about the detrimental effect of fusion upon the women in the relationship. For example, Julie Mencher has reported that many partners say the intensity of their partnership gives them significant advantages. "[C]ontrary to the idea that fusion limits the growth of individual identity, these women conveyed that the intense intimacy creates the trust and safety which foster self-actualization and risk-taking."[25] Mencher, offering an alternative to the word *fusion* as descriptive of intense and close partnerships, notes that "[e]mbeddedness as a description of healthy relational involvement acknowledges the normative developmental needs and intimacy patterns of women and revises the traditional standards of autonomy and separation which are so male-derived."[26]

Given this background, the chaplain working with Nancy and Jenny must be careful not to immediately suggest that Nancy and Jenny are fused in a manner that is destructive to their partnership. The pastoral care specialist points out that Nancy is responding to a crisis in which she accurately senses a potential loss. This is normal and common for someone dealing with life-threatening illness, even when the prognosis seems relatively positive. But there is some sense that Nancy has also realized that the covenant established between herself and Jenny has not been ultimately helpful for her in developing extended friendships and relationships, and in being honest with her children or others. It would appear that this is a case of fusion, although it does not seem to have the overtly destructive character of partners who are more controlling or who experience other dangerous behavior.

Listening carefully to Nancy as she tells the story of their partnership enables the pastoral care specialist to celebrate the depth and intensity of the relationship while also attending to the nature of the promises and pledges that have guided Nancy and Jenny in their partnership. Assuming that the love in this partnership sustains them as individuals and as partners, it is possible to engage Nancy in thinking about how that love can also encourage them to extend their relationships to others. Jenny and Nancy are probably in the latter seasons of their relationship. Utilizing this awareness means articulating with Nancy and Jenny how they have moved through conflict in the past. This rehearsal of their past, in turn, encourages them to employ the skills they learned from those experiences to deal with areas of tension that will undoubtedly arise anew as they seek loving ways to relate to others beyond the partnership.

The issues of justice are present as the chaplain attends to the ways the partnership has been established around an intentional understanding of shared power, shared opportunity, and equality in access to resources. Naming for Nancy the injustices that have caused her to feel a need to be closeted about her life may help her find the ability to transfer her sense of shared power within her primary relationship to the broader world in which she lives. Nancy has felt bound by the rules of others to the extent that she has not allowed herself the gift of sharing intimately with others about the importance of this partnership. Helping Nancy recognize that protecting one's self in the culture does not require closing off relationships from others may invite her to risk telling the truth about her partnership to some people she trusts.

Mutuality is obviously present in the relationship between Jenny and Nancy. They have worked hard to clarify the boundaries of their relationship and to protect each other's best interests in the partnership. However, once again, reframing the issue of fusion with Nancy and Jenny moves the therapeutic interpretation away from dysfunction and toward their strengths. Knowing how to be mutual with one another can help them focus on ways that they might want to become mutual with particular friends. They can choose carefully people with whom they would like to be more open, ultimately moving mutuality beyond the boundaries of the primary relationship.

The goals in working with Nancy and Jenny are:

1. *Offering Nancy and Jenny the opportunity to affirm their covenant.* It would be a mistake in this case to immediately work with Jenny and Nancy on individuation without first confirming the love, justice, and mutuality that are present in their partnership. In the process, it is important to lift up the manner in which Jenny and Nancy have already faced adversity in their partnership, and to engage them in conversations about how to build upon their past in creating a future environment of nurture and care for one another.

2. *Encouraging Jenny and Nancy to state individual needs and desires.* Nancy and Jenny have probably learned to depend upon each other and have avoided developing interests they do not share. Helping them identify individual areas of interest can assist each to clarify her needs and desires. Recognizing that it may be threatening at some levels for them to immediately move outside the relationship, the pastoral care specialist can work with Jenny and Nancy to identify feelings of being threatened that emerge as each thinks about the other moving outside the primary relationship. This process can also help Jenny and Nancy clarify the ways they are distinct from each other, and learn to affirm these differences rather than fear them. Ultimately, the development and communication of in-

dividual needs and desires will encourage them to build new patterns of relating without dismissing or ignoring the kind of intentionality that has already gone into the building of their partnership.

3. *Broadening the desire for community.* While affirming the manner in which Nancy and Jenny have become close to and intimate with each other, the caregiver should help them identify their need for others outside of the partnership. The pastoral care specialist at this point might engage Nancy and Jenny in thinking concretely about which persons they may wish to develop community with. Are they interested in a community of faith that would receive them openly or are they more interested in finding a women's community? Can they search for places to develop some of their individual interests where they might also meet new friends? The proactive pastoral caregiver will know the resources in the community that might be appropriate for Jenny and Nancy.

Nancy and Jenny provide for the pastoral care specialist an opportunity to reframe an issue that can be understood as both a strength and as a potential liability in lesbian partnerships. Building on the strength without denying the liability requires gifted and caring pastoral persons who affirm and challenge this partnership into the future.

Conclusion

Women in lesbian partnerships experience human conflicts that can be addressed best by pastoral care specialists who have developed a working knowledge of the distinctiveness of women's relationships. The mutual process of working on assessments and goals in coalition with the women in the partnership provides the appropriate care and counsel necessary for women as they nurture their relationships. The development of covenantal partnerships that embody the qualities of love, justice, and mutuality can be enhanced by pastoral care specialists who work carefully with women to support their primary relationships.

Chapter Five

Maintaining
and Extending Families

Helen and Beth live in separate residences and have been partners for a little over one year. Helen, forty-three, is a professional who works for an accounting firm and maintains a fairly middle-class standard of living. Beth, thirty-five, works as a maintenance person for a small business, earning a little over minimum wage plus benefits. Helen has two children in their late teen years who live with her most of the time. She has not confided in her children about her relationship and is very cautious around them. For example, Beth does not stay overnight when the teens are in the house. In the beginning of their partnership Helen and Beth were content just to be with each other as much as time would permit. They juggled Helen's responsibilities with the children, their respective jobs, and met mutual friends for occasional dinners or other social events.

In the past few months Beth has redeveloped a strong friendship with Joan, a woman with whom Beth was once involved. The relationship between Joan and Beth was brief, lasting about eight months, but it was also very intense. It was shortly after Joan decided that she did not want to be in relationship with Beth that Helen and Beth began seeing each other. For several months Joan and Beth did not see each other except at larger gatherings such as women's dances or parties. However, since Beth and Joan had many mutual friends, they were with each other often during social occasions. About nine months after their separation, Joan and Beth began spending more time together. Joan, self-employed and with flexible hours during the day, began meeting Beth for lunch about once a week. They now talk to one another daily on the phone and manage to spend a couple of hours together during the week. Frequently the three of them—Joan, Beth, and Helen—meet for dinner or drinks. They have begun to extend invitations to include more persons for potluck gatherings and have developed a strong network of eight or ten friends whom they refer to as "family."

At one of the recent potlucks Joan encouraged people to participate in an upcoming PRIDE rally. The community of lesbians, gay men, bisexual persons, and advocates for equal rights were having a parade and gathering at the city park to demonstrate to the city that there are many within the lesbian/gay/bisexual community who are proud of their sexual orientations and who want to be granted equality in housing, job opportunities, health benefits, and more. It would be a day of political activism with coverage by many of the local newspapers and radio and television stations. Joan was organizing some of the members of her local Affirmation group (United Methodist network for supporting and affirming lesbians/gays/bisexuals) for the march. She wanted her friends in the potluck group to participate.

Until then, Helen and Beth's relationship had seemed relatively free of conflict. However, after thinking about Joan's persuasive speech to get involved in actively demonstrating for equal rights, Beth began contemplating the parade and was thinking of participating. She wanted Helen to join her. This led to a rather intense conflict about what it would mean for them to be open, to march in the parade and to participate in the rally. Beth tried to convince Helen that it was important to participate because they deserved the same benefits as others, and it would make a statement about their relationship. Helen could only imagine the reaction of her parents, ex-husband, children, and other friends if she were seen on television as a participant in this event. They were at an impasse when they decided to seek out a third party to help them discern their course of action. The pastoral counselor they approached for assistance was related to the church that hosted the Affirmation fellowship and was open to working with them as partners.

This case represents multiple levels of "family" relationships alongside issues of coming out. The status of being "in the closet" or being "out" directly affects the relationships women have with parents, siblings, extended family, ex-spouses and ex-partners, and children. At the same time, Helen, Beth, and their friends illustrate the significance of creating "families of choice" within the lesbian community.

Three areas of concern are the focus in this chapter: first, how theological reflections on the meaning of family contribute to the conversations pastoral caregivers have with women in lesbian partnerships; second, "coming out" as a process of growing self-awareness, parallelled with choices persons make about self-disclosure of sexual orientation and identity to others; third, issues surrounding lesbian mothers and the role of "families of choice." The chapter concludes by returning to the case of Beth, Helen, and their friends, examining pastoral theological insights and clinical assessments for specialists working with women in lesbian partnerships.

Reflections on
Theology and Family

What does it mean to extend the metaphor of family to include women in lesbian relationships? "Family" refers not just to women, their parents, their siblings, and their extended relatives, but also to ex-partners, ex-spouses, children, and others whom lesbians embrace as members of their families of choice. Several definitions of family have emerged in the contemporary world, each setting norms about who is to be included and who is to be excluded in the concept of family. Definitions serve to delineate essential qualities or characteristics that make one thing different from some other thing. Power is given to those who create and maintain the normative definitions for families since they mark the boundaries of who to include and who to exclude in family structures. This is significant for those women who challenge traditional understandings and who are often excluded from normative understandings of families.

Those who seek to fortify the traditional interpretations of family usually opt for narrow boundaries. From this perspective, families are persons with whom one shares legal commitments (marriages, adoptions) or blood relationships. Some within the Judeo-Christian tradition believe that such connections "set forth the intrinsic order of this social system as grounded in the revealed purpose and will of God."[1] The rigidity of this definition results in a lack of breadth and diversity and usually does not include lesbian partnerships. In turn, most churches that operate out of narrower definitions of family do not openly welcome women in lesbian relationships and their families, or other nontraditional relationships.

Others have cast the definition of family so broadly that it, like many other metaphors, loses meaning. In this latter case families include any person with whom one feels some sense of closeness. Churches that talk about everyone being family for one another often dismiss or ignore not just the particularities of women in lesbian relationships, but those of people in other nontraditional relationships as well. The lack of any definitive statement or clarity about what constitutes family results in confusion about what makes families different from other support systems or communities.[2] Defining families too narrowly excludes diversity; defined too broadly, families lack clarity because they seem to include everyone.

The goal of this chapter is not to provide yet another definition of family, or to set forth an authoritative theology of family, or to construct a pastoral counseling model for working with families.[3] Instead, four characteristics of families are discussed in hopes that they can help inform the discussion of pastoral care with women in lesbian relationships. These four understandings arise from biblical stories, theological reflection, historical realities, and experience. Together they illuminate for pastoral care specialists the significance of lesbian families.

First, experiences and feelings arising from families of origin shape human lives. The biblical narratives rehearse the ancestry of the people of Israel, providing a liturgical declaration that God has been faithful to the fathers and mothers of the faith and will surely remain faithful to the coming generations. All persons are connected to families of origin, whether those are families into which they were born, adoptive families, families that abandon and abuse, or groups of persons not related biologically but referred to as families. Those specific relationships create memories and living realities that rest deep in the souls and psyches of human beings. Whether women enjoy their families of origin or whether they attempt to move away from them emotionally or geographically, they spend their lives dealing with the issues that emerge from having lived in a particular family context.

For women who love women, the relationships they have to their families of origin can be deeply painful. Lesbian daughters, sisters, or aunts are not always cherished, appreciated, or admired. Many parents are not aware of the sexual orientation of their lesbian daughters, creating secret worlds and a resulting emotional distance between parents and their adult children. In some families, only certain relatives are aware of a particular partnership, resulting in confusing alliances and triangles. In still other families, parents and siblings become strong supporters of lesbian partners. Whatever their stance, relatively few families of origin are neutral in their feelings toward, or their perspectives about, women who love women.

The constant tension that many lesbians experience can be framed in terms of the dynamics suggested by John Patton and Brian Childs. In their book on families, these pastoral theologians allude to "the two basic energy components of family dynamics . . . centering and moving out." The family is marked by the constant presence of "centripetal/centrifugal" tension, which serves to center persons in the context of "nuclear families" while simultaneously inviting them to engage in the outside world.[4] For many women this dynamic describes the pressure of being "caught" between loyalty to families of origin and allegiance to themselves, their identities, and their partners. Pastoral care specialists can assist women as they maneuver their way through the web of relationships and feelings that emerge in the midst of families of origin.

A second characteristic of families is that they are places of intense feelings, including anger, hurt, and pain. The triangle of Hagar, Sarah, and Abraham (Gen. 16:1–16; 21:9–21) or the conception of children through intercourse between Lot and his daughters (Gen. 19:30–38), or the rape of Tamar by her brother (2 Sam. 13:1–22) reminds us that biblical characters are not exempt from the deep tragedy of family pain. At the same time, families can be places to experience the belonging and transformation that accompanies genuine covenantal love and care. Here readers of scripture are reminded about the story of Joseph and his brothers (Genesis 41—46), or that of Mary, Martha, and Lazarus (John 11:1–12:11). The resilience persons carry inside, hoping to experience families of love and transformation in the face of disappointment or rejection, is extraordinary.

Women in lesbian relationships encounter this depth and intensity of feelings in their families of origin. Emotions surface, whether they are from the anger of damages incurred in growing up or from the experience of deep love as persons stand with one another over time. Earlier it was suggested that families participate in the process of making, keeping, breaking, and renewing covenants. Many lesbians experience rejection in their families of origin, where covenants of love, care, or trust are broken. Some families move to affirmation or acceptance, but often only after a long and circuitous path ending in a renewal of covenants between persons. The potential for intense healing or incredible destruction is present in the perceived, feared, or real responses of family members to women who openly share their lives.

Women who create families by extending their love and care to those with whom they are partnered also experience intense feelings. At times these families include children. Often families of choice include other adults who become like family to one another as they share deeply the pains and celebrations of life together. Families of choice become places where women deal with disappointments, grieve losses, seek acceptance, work toward forgiveness, and pursue meaningful connections with others.

Third, from ancient biblical texts through the realities of present-day narratives, it is clear that families are diverse in their structures, their functions, and their definitions. Observing families in the Hebrew scriptures and Greek Testament brings appreciation for the great diversity and variation in family configurations. For example, the Bible contains stories about multiple wives (Deut. 21:15), women who strike out on their own to create family (Ruth and Naomi), siblings who care for one another (Mary, Martha, and Lazarus in John 11), and single parents with children (2 Kings 4:1–7; Luke 7:11–12).[5] Not being open to such diversity can result in turning families into idolatrous structures where there appears to be only one normative way to structure families.[6]

Descriptions of families in contemporary times take on rich and multifarious dimensions. In the present culture there are single-parent families, blended families, joint-custody families, lesbian families, and families without children, as well as the more traditional dual-parent heterosexual couples with children. Herb Anderson has suggested that a "theology for the family that takes creation seriously will lead to the celebration of diversity in the structures of the family as well as in the world around us."[7] Anderson's understanding reflects families that seek to empower individuality while at the same time remaining connected. Women in lesbian relationships share in the creation of diversity through families that include partnerships without children, lesbian mothers with children from previous relationships, nuclear lesbian families where children are brought into current relationships, and families of choice where other adults are treated as sisters or brothers.

Finally, families extend over time and share intergenerational concerns. Biblical stories focus not only on the ancestors but on the generations that follow. Families are historical realities bound to one another over time. Families, communities, support groups, and close friends should not be interpreted as being synonymous with one another. A major difference between families and communities is that persons move in and out of communities without assuming that they are attached to each other in any meaningful way beyond the period of time that they share. In contrast, families carry some expectations about extended commitments over time. Lesbian families are created as persons enter into meaningful relationships with one another which they expect to maintain over time and which share intergenerational concerns.

To be an intergenerational family does not mean that every partnership must include children. Patton and Childs suggest that "caring for the generations" is an apt metaphor for pastoral care with families. They understand pastoral care to be a process of enabling persons to care for the intergenerational lives around them.[8] Lesbian partnerships without children influence the generations around them in many ways. By interacting and participating in their families of origin some women find ways to care for the previous generation in spite of fear or hurt or painful rejection. Others care for the generations by participating in covenants that provide role models for present and future generations. Women who love women care for the generations as they challenge more traditional and limited ways of understanding God's creation and its diversity.

Proactive pastoral caregivers are in a powerful position as they guide persons in theological reflection about what constitutes family. Seeking ways to join with families in their diversity means challenging the narrow definitions of family that do not reflect the richness of God's creative endeavors. Discussing with women what it means for them to participate in families of origin and to meaningfully extend their care to others can provide rich opportunities to explore biblical stories, traditional definitions, and ongoing creative revelations.

Families, Closets, and Coming Out

The case of Beth and Helen illuminates the various ways women in lesbian relationships handle their orientation identities with their families of origin, ex-partners, children, and the broader communities of which they are a part. This section begins with definitions of terms such as *coming out, closets, passing,* and *disclosure.* As the story of Helen and Beth illustrates, coming out is a process that involves deciding if, how, or when to share openly with families of origin. A discussion about the dynamics of coming out to families clarifies some pastoral concerns that arise in working with women in relationships.

Defining the Terms

Coming out, "a relational process," is the term used to talk about being open and honest with self and others about sexual identity orientation.[9] The first step of coming out is an internal one, as women begin to reckon with their issues of identity formation as outlined in the second chapter of this book. As women come out to themselves, they experience the pain and the power of what it means to self-name and self-identify as lesbians.[10]

Most women do not arrive simultaneously at the point of naming themselves as lesbians and sharing that information freely with others. More often women come to terms internally with their self-identity while selectively choosing with whom they share that information. Lesbians operate at various levels of openness with others. They may be completely open about their partnerships on some occasions and with certain people but remain cautious at other times. In the vernacular this process of sharing openly in some situations but not in others is referred to as coming out "part-way" or "half-way." To "come out of the closet completely" means to be open and honest about sexual orientation identity in every context.

Closet is a descriptive word that corresponds to the dynamics of hiding a part of one's self-identity or choosing carefully when to be open and out. When persons conceal their sexual identity orientations either from everyone or from selected audiences such as families of origin or people at work, they are "in the closet." Patricia Jung and Ralph Smith offer this description of closets:

> The facts about closets are plain. They make good hiding places. They also isolate us. Children know well the quick cover closets offer in a game of hide and seek. Kids also know how vulnerable to discovery they are once ensconced in a closet. Finally, children know well the terror of being trapped or locked in a closet. . . . In reality gay people are forced to choose between hiding from or exposing themselves to a hostile world. . . .
>
> Closets range in size and hence may be more or less suffocating. Some are so small that no whole person can live in them. In such cases the persons may have concealed from their conscious selves the truth about their sexual orientation. . . . Others can be truthful with themselves, but are shamed by heterosexism into keeping silent about who they really are. The can crouch in their closets, but have no room for others. Still others have walk-in size closets. They shroud their sexual orientations and pres-

ences in a public identity acceptable to our heterosexist world. Only a chosen few—usually other gay people or trusted friends—know their secrets. . . . They live constantly with the threat and fear of discovery.[11]

For many women, closets are familiar places. The sizes of their closets vary with the changing circumstances of life. For some, it is dangerous to be open at work, and they remain in the closet in their professional life. For others, the risk and fear of family response may be so great that they are closeted in their families of origin but open with friends and selected colleagues. The vast majority of women spend a significant part of their journeys juggling the various components of their lives, noting with whom they are out and with whom they remain in the closet.

Related to coming out and closets are two other words: *passing* and *closet-keeping*. Persons who pass are those who, for a variety of reasons, do not appear to be lesbian and so others assume that they are heterosexual. Women in lesbian relationships may pass by being particularly conscious of their dress or style of clothing, or they may pass by maintaining other facades that lead persons to think they are heterosexual. For example, some women pass by talking about men they are interested in dating. In some situations women who are lesbian pass by maintaining heterosexual marriages.[12] Living a "double life" or maintaining a secret identity is often undertaken when the cost of coming out seems to be greater than the hoped-for liberation of being open.

The function of maintaining secrets, closet-keeping, is taken on by persons or institutions who have information about another's sexual identity, keeping the promise of confidentiality.[13] Closet-keepers can be sisters or parents who keep the secret from other family members, or they can be friends who maintain silence in appropriate places, such as at church, around family members, or at work. Closet-keeping results in some persons having powerful secrets about others. Denominational and church leaders who encourage the maintenance of secrecy by the "don't ask, don't tell" policy reinforce the power of those who keep the secrets of those in the closets. These policies serve to fortify the closets in which women live by sending a message that they would prefer that women live in closets. In turn, this makes it more difficult for women to come out and be open.

Self-disclosure, discovery, and *outing* are the terms most often used to talk about some part of the process of coming out. Unlike other groups who are not part of the dominant culture and who might be identified by the color of their skin, it is possible for women in lesbian partnerships to be invisible to those who choose not to see. Heterosexuality is often presumed by the dominant culture, meaning that persons must consciously disclose their identities if they are to be seen.[14] Self-disclosure implies that lesbians have the power to choose the timing of their coming out, maintaining control over who knows and who does not know the fullness of their identities and orientations.

Sometimes a person does not have the opportunity to self-disclose and she is "discovered" to be lesbian. For example, a parent going through old boxes in the basement may find letters written to the daughter from another woman, or congregations may suspect someone in leadership is lesbian when people outside the congregation indiscriminately talk about the woman. Discovery can be traumatic to those who have been living fairly closeted lives, for they have not had the time to prepare themselves or others for their self-disclosure. As a result the discovery takes more people by surprise, including the lesbians involved.

Outing has become a controversial political strategy within the lesbian and gay community. Those who choose some kind of public medium (lesbian newspapers, gay activist rallies, books or articles) to identify others as being lesbian or gay participate in the process of outing others. They decide it is more important to make someone's lesbian identity public knowledge than to allow that individual the right to make choices about her own coming out process. The persons most often selected for outing are public figures who previously have not been open. There is debate within the lesbian and gay community about the ethics of outing. One opinion can be articulated in this way: "Outing entails the violation of an at least implicit request that we treat the knowledge of an individual's sexual identity as confidential."[15] Others suggest that outing is an ethical response based upon the conviction that those who are silent are betraying not only themselves but others within the community. The adage that "silence is death" conveys the sentiment of those who believe that it is the moral responsibility of lesbians and gay men to be open about their sexual identities.[16]

Coming out is, in reality, both an individual and a communal process. As an individual process persons make choices about their openness. Psychotherapists and others debate about whether it is healthier for women to live openly or whether a woman can maintain secrecy about her orientations without negatively affecting her mental health. Psychiatrist Nanette Gartrell argues that coming out is the most healthy, if not the only, response lesbians can make to their orientations. From her perspective, it is mandatory that care specialists explore with lesbian women the benefits of coming out because being open improves "psychological well-being." She notes: "being out is necessary for healthy adaptation to lesbian life. I have found from my clinical and personal experience that self-esteem and self-image is enhanced in direct proportion to increasing visibility and openness about one's lesbianism."[17] In exploring this issue she notes that those who live in closets usually "have developed a system of defenses that allows them to function as if being closeted were ego-syntonic." In other words, Gartrell argues that the benefits of being out far exceed the benefits of juggling the closets at emotional cost.[18]

Revealing their identities as lesbians can be powerful and liberating for women in lesbian partnerships. According to some, the process of self-disclosure "of lesbian identity functions to support that identity and to promote commitment to it."[19] As lesbians identify themselves to others, they take on added power and strength in their convictions about who they are. Gartrell notes that the risks associated with coming out are often related to a generalized fear that may be unrealistic or unfounded. Consequently, from her perspective the risks and fears do not outweigh the realistic benefits of living an open and honest life. "The constant need to lie, to be on guard, and to pretend heterosexuality must be understood by clients in terms of the toll on psychic energy and injury to self-esteem."[20]

Patricia Jung and Ralph Smith suggest that living in the closet results in "sexual inauthenticity." As such, persons who choose to live in the closet put pressure and strain on their primary relationships because of withdrawal from other friends, families, or communities who may not approve of their lesbianism. While they maintain that there is a difference between lies and secrets, Jung and Smith ultimately suggest that the value of openness and sexual authenticity far outweighs the value of the closet.[21] Others recommend that it is important to test whether some women's hesitancy to self-disclose is based upon internalized homophobia or legitimate and realistic fears.[22]

Pastoral care specialists must recognize that, ultimately, coming out is a contextual matter. Each woman should be given the power to make her own choices given the circumstances of her life. Caregivers can engage their parishioners and clients in assessing the risks, the fears, and the potential benefits of either remaining in the closet or coming out. It is almost impossible for the straight pastoral caregiver to understand the depth of fear involved in coming out. Often the anxiety of being abandoned, rejected, or actively discriminated against by families, friends, church communities, or colleagues in work settings is greater than most heterosexual counselors can anticipate or understand. Added to this is the reality that, while at an intellectual or rational level women may have pondered the meaning of their coming out, there are feelings and emotions that accompany the process that can't be predicted. The feelings are important to accept, understand, and appreciate because they mark the depth of significance for women who claim lesbian identities.

Other factors that should be considered in relation to the coming out process include the timing of the self-disclosure and other dynamics operative in a particular woman's family of origin. Decision making about coming out may be related to other crises. For example, it is not unusual for women to choose to self-disclose their lesbian identities at the moment when there is significant stress in the primary partnership. Some women choose not to tell others until they are in the midst of grieving a lost relationship, job, or career and are in need of support and care. Still others are more likely to tell during the initial excitement of a new lover. Other lesbian partners decide to be more open as they struggle to make decisions about adding children to their partnerships.[23] Particular events can affect when, how, and to whom lesbians self-disclose.

Significant issues to consider in conversations about coming out to families of origin can include such things as the age or health of parents. For example, some women choose to tell parents just before they are lost in death. Others recognize that revealing their identity to a parent may be more than the parent can handle emotionally. A pastoral colleague suggested that signs of justice in the process of making choices about self-disclosure can involve consideration for the well-being of those who are even more vulnerable than the one who is coming out.[24] This caution does not mean that decisions about coming out should be made solely on the basis of how others might feel or how others will react. Instead, what is suggested is the recognition that decisions to come out have an impact on persons outside the context of the primary partnerships, and these other persons ought also to be taken into consideration since coming out is a relational process.

There is a communal side to the process of coming out. As noted earlier, Jung and Smith suggest that openness about being lesbian is a way of living sexually authentic lives in the midst of community.[25] In a similar vein, Carter Heyward notes that being open and coming out make a theological statement about being in faithful and mutual communal relationships: "To come out as a lesbian or gayman is to make our sexuality a (possibly the) central factor in our public world. To come out without realizing this is irresponsible."[26] Those who live in closets deny to the community around them the opportunity of knowing them and learning from them about liberation and life.[27]

From this communal perspective coming out is a process of liberation and empowerment not just for lesbians and their partners but also for the community. Coming out is a political act that upsets the status quo and moves the world off center. Those who intentionally choose to come out to self and others serve as a catalyst for those lesbians and gay men who may be at an earlier point in the journey or who are on the verge of being more open about their lives.[28] The truth is that the more lesbians who are out of the closet about their sexual orientations, the greater the potential is for families, communities of faith, and others to work toward the affirmation of women in lesbian partnerships as whole and faithful persons.

J. Michael Clark, in a powerful book titled *A Place to Start*, suggests that coming out should be more than an option persons have in community; rather, coming out is essential to the community itself. "Coming out is, thus, not only an intensely personal act, but a social, political, and spiritual act as well."[29] Writing as a gay man, Clark's thesis is that lesbians and gay men must "claim and use our power to effect liberation; and claiming our power means we must first (re)claim and (re)affirm ourselves. Only in claiming ourselves, in coming out, do we really begin to glimpse the immense power we actually have."[30] As part of a communal process of liberation, those who come out participate in the ongoing movements toward liberation and justice for all.

Coming out is not something that should be prescribed. Instead, women in lesbian relationships ought to be invited into thinking through their own processes and decision making. For some, being open takes a lifetime to negotiate. For others, coming out is a process that happens quickly. Because coming out is a relational process that takes courage and fortitude, women need to be allowed to make their own way as they choose. There is considerable pressure from inside the lesbian and gay community for persons to come out. Often those who have chosen to live their lives openly have little memory of the fear that they experienced while living in their closets. Pastoral caregivers should work slowly and intentionally with clients, encouraging women to be responsible for their choices, taking the time they need to decide about the size of their closets or the openness of their lives. Coming out will depend upon the contextual lives of those women with whom they work.

Coming Out to Families

Families of origin are places that often hold the greatest intensity of feelings in terms of the coming out process. Again, the stories range from women whose families have been supportive and proactive in working toward eradicating heterosexism to those whose parents or relatives exclude them from the family, write them out of their wills, ask them never to return, or threaten them with serious injury.[31] In between the extremes are the numerous families who find dealing with lesbians and their partners to be confusing, painful, promising, and healing. The mixture of reactions is matched only by the richness of personal and familial journeys. Families are not predictable when dealing with lesbians and their partners. There are, however, some factors to keep in mind when offering care to women in lesbian partnerships.

First, coming out to families of origin touches off feelings of grief that may emerge both in the women who are self-disclosing and in their parents or family members. For lesbians there is the loss of previous ways of relating to members of the family. Even when those patterns have been stressful or unhealthy, they were at least predictable and somewhat comfortable. Coming out means those who are self-disclosing lose something, even if it is the smallness of the closet in which they have lived. For some women in lesbian partnerships grief surfaces as they recognize they will never be accepted in their families of origin in the same way as are their

siblings and spouses. The sadness that accompanies the internal or external losses women experience should not be interpreted as a grief about being lesbians, but as a recognition that change means loss.[32]

Grief is also present as parents and other relatives mourn the loss of images or visions they had of their daughters, sisters, or nieces. Feeling caught
off guard and that they do not really know the person who self-discloses,
family members may express their grief in confusing ways. It is important
to remember that each family processes loss in its own way.[33] Parents do
not always name loss as their first reaction, and the immediate feelings expressed by family members may not look like the kind of grief we normally
associate with losing someone or something.[34] Instead, grief may be expressed as anger or deep hurt. Hence, pastoral caregivers in this situation
can be extremely helpful as they listen attentively and name the grief in a
way that gives it honor. Framing feelings as grief and loss can take the initial hurt away from other more negative reactions sometimes expressed by
family members.

Some parents also experience the grief of losing faith in what Mary
Borhek defines as a "fundamental belief" that all persons are "born heterosexual unless they are sick, neurotic, rebellious, or perverse."[35] It is
common for parents to assume more responsibility than is deserved, thinking that they have somehow "caused" their children to be lesbians. Initially
the feelings of guilt or failure may be overwhelming. Some parents react
by being intensely angry or confused; others state that they never want to
talk about the subject again; still others express the mixed reaction of saying they accept their daughters but think that their daughters will never be
happy. There are times when

> [f]amilial rejection and accompanying loss is often much more subtle
> and disguised than . . . outright discarding. . . . Because of its subtlety,
> however, it is often much more damaging to the psyche. Couching ex-
> pressions of rejection in loving terms confuses people and sets up a sys-
> tem of "crazy-making."[36]

Parents and family members cope with changing the images they have of
their relatives who are lesbian in various ways. Pastoral caregivers who assist women as they move through their feelings about family reactions can
be extremely helpful not only to the women in partnerships but ultimately
to their families of origin.

A second factor in counseling women concerning coming out is to help
them recognize that being open in families takes incredible time and energy. The initial disclosure may take only a few moments, but the emotional preparations by women who self-disclose have probably taken considerably longer. Likewise, the response to self-disclosure and the ongoing
dialogue within families often spans months or years. Because of the emo-

tional intensity women expect from their families of origin, family members are often told one at a time "with the emotionally closest member being told first."[37]

On occasions women choose to tell everyone in their families of origin all at once, but the more likely case scenario is for women to test one person's response before putting other family relationships in jeopardy. Often siblings are the first persons in the family with whom women in lesbian partnerships are open and honest. According to Kath Weston's study reported in *Families We Choose*, siblings are more accepting of same-sex partnerships than are parents.[38] Parents have an emotional and internal investment in who their children become that siblings do not carry. As a result, there is more potential for disappointment or hurt on the part of everyone as parents struggle to discern the meaning of their daughters' lesbian identities.

Self-disclosure in families creates tension in established patterns of relationships within the families themselves. It is common for self-disclosure by someone in the family to result in new kinds of bonding within the systemic structures of the family.[39] Sometimes self-disclosure in families strengthens alliances between particular members of the families. As Sherry Zitter notes, family coalitions can shift when women come out to their families of origin. In particular, Zitter cites changes in the mother-daughter relationship as mothers come to terms with new understandings of their daughters and themselves. In some families this may be the first time that a daughter stands over against her parents in such a direct manner, causing a disturbance of the previous balance operative in the family. Object relations theory suggests that self-disclosure can be a movement toward differentiation and can signal an important event for changing the dynamics between mothers and daughters.[40]

Assisting parishioners and clients to think about the systems of which they are a part, of their family triangles, and of the impact of their self-disclosure upon those relationships is an essential part of working with women in lesbian relationships. While it is impossible to predict the reaction of parents or other family members, it is helpful to anticipate some of their potential feelings.

A third factor in counseling lesbians concerned with coming out to families is to assist them to think about the differences between their culture as lesbian women and the culture of their parents. Occasionally a lesbian has a parent who is also lesbian or gay, but more often the culture about which lesbians speak is distinct from that of their parents, for whom it often carries negative images. As a result, stereotypes and myths may appear in the initial reactions and statements that parents or siblings make as they respond to the announcement from women about their lesbian orientations and/or their partnerships.[41] As Erik Strommen points out, the negative conception that some parents have of lesbian lifestyles will have a direct impact on their initial reactions. Hence, they respond to the self-disclosure out of their assumptions about a community that they do not know well.[42] Women who love women must be willing to walk with their parents, siblings, and others as they educate and teach them about the culture of which they are a part.

Pastoral care specialists can be proactive in working with women as they think about how to care for themselves in the midst of potential negative family reactions. One way to work with women in lesbian partnerships is to elicit from them the presuppositions, moral stances, or beliefs about homosexuality they suspect their parents to have. Talking about these myths can help women frame some possible responses to their families. Offering reading materials to take to family members or suggesting that lesbians think of persons who might talk to their family members about their feelings can be gentle reminders of the need to care even as persons are confronted with the truth. Women should not feel obligated to teach their parents about being lesbian. At the same time, the qualities of love, justice, and mutuality might best be served by a willingness on the part of lesbian partners to share as much as is safe with their families. In addition, pastoral care specialists who work in the church and community to educate others assist in opening the doors for ongoing conversations between lesbians and their families. The more pastoral caregivers help churches to deal with the issue of women in lesbian partnerships before persons have to respond to the self-disclosure of women, the greater the potential for reconciliation and healing in the process of women coming out to their families.

Finally, as women come out to their families, old family wounds may be touched and reopened. Past sexual abuse, alcoholism, severe family dysfunction, or other issues may reemerge in response to the disclosure, thereby complicating the process for the families as well as for the women who have risked coming out.[43] In families where sexuality has not been talked about openly, members may experience shame or guilt in openly discussing something that previously has been avoided.[44] The manner in which families dealt with conflicts in the past will affect how they now deal with the discovery or self-disclosure of lesbian women. Strommen notes the importance of attending to "the conflict resolution mechanisms available to the family members."[45] Pastoral care specialists will find it helpful to work with women on the patterns their families have developed to deal with conflict, assisting them to plan their coming out in a way that will provide them with liberation rather than increased long-term pain.

For some women, coming out to their families of origin is best handled through open and honest conversation with the entire nuclear family. Others, as noted above, will come out to some individuals within the family before everyone knows. Some women first present their story in letters and wait for a response before talking openly and in person with their families.

There is no right approach to coming out that is appropriate for all women and their families. Particular contexts will summon forth individual ways of moving through the process.

Pastoral caregivers should be aware that coming out to families of origin means that the families, in turn, move through a parallel process of coming out. Strommen delineates a five-stage process families often move through in coming to terms with the discovery or self-disclosure of lesbians. In the first stage families may intuitively sense that a child or sibling is lesbian. This "subliminal awareness" may be the result of subtle hints given by women to their families, or of family members' instinctive knowledge. The second stage includes the disclosure and initial reactions by family members. Here the feelings may be intense as families struggle to regain their balance. This is followed by a third stage, a period of adjustment. Initially after hearing the news there may be a "crisis atmosphere," which gives way to an urging "to change orientation or to keep the homosexual identity a secret, thus maintaining respectability for the family."[46]

In the fourth stage, resolution, family members move through the grief process outlined above and work to change some of their previously held negative images about lesbian women. Women in lesbian partnerships may serve as educators or mentors as they challenge the negative assumptions of their family members. In this stage churches can be proactive as they engage persons in thinking through the moral, biblical, and theological issues that emerge as families respond to the lesbian identities of their daughters or siblings. The eventual journey can lead to Strommen's fifth stage, "integration, in which a new role for the child and new behaviors for dealing with the child's gay identity are enacted."[47]

Families may stop at any stage during the process, or particular family members may have a more difficult time than others moving from one stage to another. Pastoral care specialists should be aware of this process in working with lesbians and ought to explore the dynamics of the family with women in the context of counseling. Women need to be reminded that initial family reactions will not necessarily be the final position of family members. First responses are often temporary, changing over time.

As families come to terms with the lesbian identity of a family member, they must make choices about their own coming out process, such as whom they wish to tell about their lesbian relative. For example, when a woman comes out to her parents and siblings, they must then decide who else to inform within the context of the extended family. This may cause conflict when persons disagree on the extent of the disclosure. Some parents or siblings may want to keep the secret and not tell others, while the lesbian partners may want to be included openly in the next family reunion or holiday venture. Negotiating these decisions within the context of the extended family often takes ongoing conversation and time.

Family members may live in their own closets, fearing the response or reactions of others. They must decide whether they would like to come out to others such as church friends, colleagues, or long-time family friends. Many families feel that they cannot disclose the lifestyles and orientations of their respective lesbian family members because they will be rejected by their communities of faith or be seen as less-than-adequate parents. Family members must think about how to handle questions about their children that, prior to the self-disclosure, may not have seemed as important. For example, questions about an adult child and her future plans for marriage or children might be met by internal reactions of fear, guilt, or shame on the part of parents or other family members.[48]

Various configurations of family members can be involved in the coming out process. In the story of Helen and Beth the traditional nuclear families are present (parents and siblings) alongside Helen's ex-husband and teenage children. Women who are in heterosexual marriages and who come out to themselves as lesbian have a more complex process as they make choices about the status of their marriages in addition to whether they come out to their husbands.[49] In similar ways, choosing how, when, or if to tell children becomes an issue for many women. Custody battles can be fought over issues of a woman's sexual orientation if she chooses to be open and if the dynamics of the custody situation are volatile.[50] As a result, women may choose not to tell their children for fear that their relationships with them might be lost. Studies are beginning to emerge on the reactions of various groups to the self-disclosure of lesbian identity. Ex-husbands, for example, may react as if they are responsible in some way for the lesbian identity of the ex-wives, thinking that if they had been better husbands their ex-wives would not have chosen to love women.[51]

Finally, added to these complexities is the fact that most lesbian partnerships are formed by two women, each of whom is likely to be in a different place in the process of coming out. As illustrated in the case study that begins this chapter, Helen and Beth each bring expectations, hopes, and visions to this issue of what it means to be closeted or open. Assisting women to negotiate the differences between them can be one of the greatest gifts offered by pastoral care specialists. Engaging partners in choosing their own liberating strategy can empower women like Beth and Helen to gain clarity about how to proceed, recognizing the tensions and anxieties that emerge in their relationship in the process. Encouraging women to voice their feelings can be healing as women come to understand the intricacy of their life together. Noting that women may not find themselves instantly happier once they come out, but reminding them that their perceptions and feelings will shift with time, are ways of being pastoral with lesbian partners who are moving through the process of coming out.

Lesbian Families of Choice

In the previous chapters of this book I have focused almost exclusively on the women involved in lesbian partnerships. Now, however, I will briefly consider other persons within lesbian families of choice such as children and others who relate in a manner of extended "kinship" as if they were family.

Lesbian Mothers

Lesbian mothers may be women from traditional heterosexual relationships whose children were part of their prior relationships with men, or women who choose to bring children into their established lesbian partnerships through adoption, alternative insemination, or sexual intercourse with a male for the sole purpose of procreation.[52] Three categories of lesbian families include children:

nuclear, with children who are born to or adopted by the couple; *blended*, where children are included who came originally from their mother's prior relationship (usually with a man); and *extra-blended*, where children come from both sources.[53]

The concerns of lesbian mothers are many, including challenges with legal systems and self-disclosure issues.

Motherhood crosses orientation lines and includes both straight and lesbian women. In some ways being a lesbian mother says more about what it means to be a mother in our culture than it does about what it means to be a lesbian. Ellen Lewin, who interviewed 135 mothers, 73 who were lesbian and 62 who were single heterosexual mothers, suggests "not that lesbian mothers resemble heterosexual mothers in a way that minimizes the importance of their lesbianism but that lesbian mothers, like other mothers, share in the system of meaning that envelops motherhood in our culture."[54] Lesbian motherhood bridges the cultures between women who love women and women who love men. Consequently, mothers in lesbian relationships connect with the straight world in ways that they would not were there no children in the primary partnership.[55]

On the one hand, this crossing of orientation lines adds strength to friendships between lesbian and straight women as they participate together in school events, attend parent-teacher conferences, and move through some of the developmental crises typical of children and youth. On the other hand, being a lesbian mother often means that a woman feels as if she is navigating between two identities, neither of which fits her completely. The result is a sense of isolation. Sally Crawford notes that women in such situations often feel caught between at least two worlds, and their whole self may not get acknowledged in either place. It often happens that a lesbian gets her major support for the mother part of herself from straight people who cannot understand or relate to the depth of the significance of her lesbianism. At the same time, she may get major support for her lesbian self from the lesbian community, where there is less understanding of the depth of the impact of becoming a mother on her person and life.[56]

Lesbian mothers may not feel completely at home in either the lesbian world or the world of heterosexual mothers. The lesbian community is not as child-oriented as the heterosexual community since there are fewer women in lesbian partnerships who have children.[57] This should not suggest that children are not welcome in the lesbian community, but it may mean that women who love women and who have children may have to be more vocal about their issues and needs within the community.

Cultural norms about procreation affect lesbian and straight mothers differently. Unlike straight women who have to contend with questions about why they are not mothers, lesbians often are confronted with a kind of "compulsory childlessness," the assumption that they are not interested in or capable of being good mothers.[58] It is assumed that good heterosexual marriages produce children unless some physical reason prevents couples from conceiving. The opposite premise holds true for women who self-identify as lesbians. Many people outside the lesbian community wonder aloud about bringing children into families of lesbian partnerships.

The cultural bias that lesbians are either not interested in children or do not make good mothers merges with the realistic fears of women in lesbian partnerships that their children will be taken away from them should others discover their partnership. The courts have been known to assume that children raised by lesbian partners are negatively affected in their mental, emotional, or sexual development. Similarly, some have argued that children and youth who are reared by lesbian parents may be stigmatized or rejected by their peers. While it is true that in both the heterosexual and the lesbian community some parents are more capable than others, it is not clear that children raised by lesbians have deeper or more distressing experiences in childhood or in their teen years. Nor can it be asserted that children raised in lesbian homes have an abnormal understanding of their sexuality.[59]

Many lesbian mothers risk losing their children should their lesbian relationships become public. Patricia Falk notes that in the legal system, once the issue shifts from the welfare of the children or youth to the self-identity of lesbian mothers, the biases of the culture work against lesbians.[60] Whether their children come from a previous heterosexual marriage or whether they are adopted, women in lesbian relationships may typically experience appropriate fear and distrust of the legal system. The fear quite often leads to invisibility as lesbians. Instead of claiming their self-identities as lesbian mothers, many women are perceived in the culture as straight single parents.[61] The invisibility is one way of protecting themselves from judges who would grant custody to others purely on the basis of the mothers' lesbian relationships. At the same time, this invisibility reinforces isolation and fear in women and their partners.

Weston offers these words of insight from her research on lesbian and gay families: "Descriptively speaking, the categories of gay kinship might better be labeled families we struggle to create, struggle to choose, struggle to legitimate, and—in the case of blood or adoptive family—struggle to keep."[62] Since the legal systems are often biased against lesbian mothers, the struggle to keep children and the realistic fear of losing them if women are out and open needs to be considered carefully by the pastoral care specialist who is working with lesbian mothers, their partners, and their children.

Blended families include partnerships where children were born before the current lesbian relationship was formed. These children can be the result of a traditional heterosexual marriage or relationship, or they can be children conceived or adopted in the context of a former lesbian partnership. Issues of coming out for women who have previously been in heterosexual relationships are particularly complex. First, as noted above, the fear of legal custody battles often works against women in lesbian partnerships and in their striving to be open. Since there is usually a biological father who may or may not know of the self-identity of the lesbian mother, women may fear that fathers will distort and negatively use the information about their ex-partners in the context of custody battles.[63] A second issue is raised as women discern how to come out to children or youth once they decide it is safe to be open with them. D. Merilee Clunis and G. Dorsey Green suggest the following guidelines for women who are thinking about coming out to their children:

> Sort out your own feelings about being a lesbian first. . . . Reassure your children that your sexual partnership does not change your relationship with them or your feelings for them. . . . Be prepared to answer questions. . . . Be prepared for your child to withdraw for a while. . . . Stay calm.[64]

Children and youth, who are sometimes uncomfortable with their own sexuality, may experience an increase in anxiety when dealing with the sexual orientation of a lesbian mother. Young people must not only deal with the homophobic or sexist attitudes of the culture but also come to terms with their own feelings about what it means to have a mother who loves another woman, particularly if that is a new image of their mother. Older children and youth who have had longer socialization periods in traditional heterosexual families may need more time and assistance in adjusting to the realities of being mothered by lesbians. Several authors suggest that the younger a child is while the mother is in the process of coming out, the easier it is for the child to accept and to deal with the lesbian identity of the mother and the reactions of peers.[65]

Lesbian mothers who talk openly with their children and youth about sharing this information with others provide clarity as children and youth move through their own coming out process. For example, lesbian mothers need to remain attentive to potential triangulation if they confide in their children or youth but do not want them to share that information with the other parent. Some youth are caught in the precarious position of keeping secrets from a father in an effort to protect a mother. Pastoral caregivers must be willing to work with children and youth as they come to terms with what it means to be part of a lesbian-mothered household.

Women in lesbian partnerships who are in the process of expanding their families by bringing children into the relationship through adoption or birth must contend with other issues. Crawford notes that women are tempted to idealize and romanticize what it means to raise children in lesbian partnerships.[66] This does not mean lesbian partners should not seek ways to include children in their partnerships; rather, it means that like all women who are thinking of having children they need to be counseled about the realities, the risks, the joys, and the hopes that they foresee in bringing children into their families.

As women move toward making decisions about having children, factors to be explored include the economic status of a partnership, its longevity, and its stability. Bringing children into lesbian partnerships highlights class issues as women determine the manner for bringing children into their families.[67] Alternative insemination requires financial and medical resources that may not be available to all women. Adoptions, on the other hand, are often difficult for women because some agencies are not open to placing children in lesbian partnerships. For some, private or special adoptions are the avenues for placing children in their homes. Even here, however, they must contend with court systems that may take children from their home if they are discovered to be lesbians. Others may find a male (perhaps a relative of the other partner or a friend) who is willing to participate in sexual intercourse for the purpose of procreation. In this case there are legal and practical considerations to be considered as part of the counseling process. Questions about what rights or obligations the male has in relationship to the child and the partnership should be dealt with before insemination occurs.[68]

Co-parenting as mothers is an exciting and challenging process that creates particular tensions within the partnership. As noted above, lesbian families are sometimes invisible in the culture. In most contexts one mother has to be named as the official or legal parent. As one author notes: "The fact that there is *legally* one 'real' mother reinforces the psychological tendency to *perceive* only one 'real' mother."[69] Many lesbian partnerships have difficulty in being viewed by those around them as legitimate co-parents. The partnership may experience increased stress as one woman becomes identified as the "other" parent but not the legal mother. Added to these complexities are the normal processes of mothers discovering themes from their respective families of origin which emerge and sometimes create conflicts between parents.[70] With those who are thinking about bringing children into lesbian families, the issues of the partnerships should be discussed openly and with care.

Finally, a word needs to be stated clearly about those partners who, for a variety of reasons, do not have children as part of their family structure. Weston, in her work on families, notes that

> [w]hat gay kinship ideologies challenge is not the concept of procreation that informs kinship in the U.S., but the belief that procreation *alone* constitutes kinship, and that "nonbiological" ties must be patterned after a biological model (like adoption) or forfeit any claim to kinship status.[71]

Women who love women do not need to have children in order to participate in the intergenerational concerns lifted earlier in this chapter. Judith Plaskow, a Jewish feminist theologian, offers some interesting concepts about sexuality and procreation in a book titled *Twice Blessed: On Being Lesbian or Gay and Jewish:*

> [J]ust as Judaism has always recognized that procreation does not exhaust the meaning of sexuality, so having children does not exhaust the ways in which Jews can contribute to future generations. . . . The sense of integrity and self-worth that a loving sexual relationship can foster enhances the capacity to make commitments to the future, whether this takes the form of bearing and raising children or nurturing communal continuity in other ways.[72]

Thus, having children is not the only way to influence future generations. As children—nieces and nephews and children of friends, relatives, and others—watch women in lesbian partnerships living out covenants of love, justice, and mutuality, new visions of the future take shape.

Lesbian Extended Families

Lesbian families may or may not include children, but they almost always include other adults who function as family. It is common in the lesbian community to refer to other lesbians and gay men with whom one is close as being "families of choice." Weston notes from her anthropological study that talking about families within the lesbian and gay men's communities often illuminates a more flexible idea of family than is found within traditionally heterosexual communities. In the "families they [are] fashioning" women who love women find the support, strength, and love that they may not experience in their families of origin.[73]

Extended families of choice embody the features suggested in the theological reflections earlier in this chapter. Women in lesbian partnerships who have extended families of choice still contend with issues from their families of origin. The created family cannot replace the experiences and impact of those original families in which persons were raised. Within extended families of choice there are deep and intense feelings. Women are bound together over time and expect to remain faithful family members for one another even when covenants of particular relationships may shift.

Diversity is present as families of choice extend across household lines. Persons considered as family can be those with whom there is a shared history, or those who have been emotionally or economically supportive of one another. Women who do not share common living space may still consider themselves to be families of choice. Intergenerational concerns are lifted up as extended families stand together over time and join in providing new ways of being in relationships for future generations. The fluid reality of extended families of choice does not mean that there are no boundaries; rather, it suggests that women who love women find creative and diverse ways of extending their families of love, justice, and mutuality.

Among women in lesbian relationships it is not unusual to find former lovers remaining as part of extended families of choice, even when one of the women in the former partnership establishes a new relationship. The story of Helen, Beth, and Joan is not unusual. Former partners remain steadfast friends for a number of reasons.

First, as Jo-Ann Krestan and Claudia Bepko suggest, former lovers "may represent attempts to evolve substitute family networks."[74] Families of choice are created as women bring other persons closer for reasons of support and care. Former lovers are not necessarily problematic to new relationships; rather they often function as family members might in other heterosexual contexts. Ex-partners may be persons with whom women talk about their new relationships or struggles and pains in an existing partnership.

Second, in many places the network of lesbians may be relatively small or confined. Large cities have many lesbians who often associate within established subsystems. Each network has women who share friendships. Together they create normative understandings for relating within the particular system. Former lovers often see one another at social events and remain good friends, especially when they share a common subsystem.

Third, the kinship system for lesbians includes former lovers because of the strength of the friendships established in the lesbian community. As Weston notes, families of choice become extensions of friendship rather than mere reflections of sexual partners or lovers. Deep friendships result in relationships that function as families of choice.[75] Women in lesbian relationships often change the nature of their covenants, ending sexual relationship but remaining deep and long-lasting friends.

Women who love women do not casually shift from one relationship to another as is sometimes assumed by the straight community. However, as with heterosexuals, women do choose sometimes to end a particular covenantal partnership. As noted above, one of the common times for women to come out to others is when they are experiencing a change in a previous covenant or the loss of a relationship. Although the lack of a social contract or religious ceremony may give the impression that it is easy for lesbians to move away from a partnership, pastoral caregivers must be careful not to minimize the breakups of lesbian partnerships. Lesbian relationships have an emotional intensity that normally makes changing the nature of the covenant stressful. Recognizing that the relationship was important opens the door for many women to move toward healing.

There are many other ways a pastoral caregiver can be helpful. Issues raised by inequities in terms of financial resources may need discussion. Dividing material possessions bought under particular assumptions about money can cause tremendous pain when women change the status of their partnerships. Because of the fluid nature of lesbian relationships, women often move in together before they have adequately tested the stability of the relationship or worked through some of the financial matters. When it comes time to change the living arrangements or the nature of the relationship, there are few resources to assist in the process. Heterosexual couples often turn to the courts during divorce in order to settle matters, but few lesbian partnerships depend upon that type of resource. Hence, pastoral counselors may provide important services or may refer them to mediators during this emotionally charged event as former partners break up and change the nature of their covenants. Assisting them to move toward embracing each other as extended family can be helpful.

Women in lesbian partnerships need pastoral caregivers who bring the theological resources of the community of faith into their changes in relationship. Those whom lesbians consider to be their families of choice continue to illuminate the "tale of lesbians and gay men moving out of isolation and into kinship."[76] Pastoral care specialists who join women in the process of nurturing families are those who share in creating a world of greater love, justice, and mutuality.

Pastoral Care with Beth and Helen

Building upon the reflections on family in this chapter, it is possible to consider a pastoral theological approach to Beth and Helen as they seek help at this stage in their partnership. While there are many issues a pastoral care specialist may want to explore with Helen and Beth, it is helpful to return to the four characteristics articulated in the theological reflections. Ultimately the goal of a pastoral care specialist is to support and nurture the covenantal partnership by strengthening the embodiment of love, justice, and mutuality in the relationship.

First, Beth and Helen each have families of origin who appear in the context of their stories. The case study reveals less about Beth's family of origin than about Helen's. A pastoral caregiver will want to explore with Beth her own story and how her family members responded to her lesbian identity. Using the story of Beth and her family as a reference point, it is then possible to talk about Helen's decisions in coming out to her family. Beth's story should not be used as a pattern for Helen, but as a way of linking their lives together in some fashion. For example, assisting Beth to remember any fears she faced in her self-disclosure to her family of origin can do two things. First, recalling the story encourages Beth to remember that coming out is a "relational process" and that all persons move through that process differently and in their own ways. Those who are far removed from the experience of coming out sometimes forget the fear and anguish that goes into making the decisions. Second, hearing Beth's story may invite Helen to identify some of the real and generalized fears she is having about her own family. Together they can find ways to affirm and support their partnership as they connect with each other's individual fears and hopes.

Second, intense feelings are emerging within this partnership, and presumably within their families of origin and their blended family. The feelings are probably as deep, confusing, painful, and rich as any pastoral caregiver can imagine. There appears to be much genuine care between Beth, Helen, and their friends. Their family of choice seems to provide them with support, nurture, and challenge. In addition, there are the feelings Helen has for her family of origin and for those whom she has known over time. Thinking about possible responses from her ex-husband might also be raising particular anxieties and concerns. Added to this are the feelings she must be having for her children and concerns about their responses to her sexuality. A pastoral caregiver who can assist Beth and Helen in naming some of those feelings for themselves can help them clarify how they want to approach the process of their coming out. A significant piece of the pastoral work may be allowing Beth and Helen to express their feelings without being overwhelmed by their intensity.

Third, there is great diversity in the structures of the families represented in this case. Pastoral caregivers should note the varieties of connections that are apparent. The use of genograms that are creative in charting lesbian partnerships can assist Beth and Helen in claiming the different ways that they have come to think about their lesbian family. Connections between Helen, Beth, and the children must be articulated carefully. How do Helen and Beth want to present themselves to Helen's children? Are they thinking of themselves as co-mothers, or are they giving major responsibility to Helen for the children? If the latter is true, how do they adjudicate the relationship of Beth with the children? The family of choice presents another kind of richness and diversity. Those within the potluck group who operate as family of choice for Beth and Helen need to be placed on the diagram in a way that honors their relationships with one another.

Fourth, Beth and Helen along with Joan and their friends are in the process of creating new visions for present and future generations. They are caring for the generations of the past as they think together about what it means to have been raised in their families of origin and how to remain connected with those families. Similarly, as they think about participating in the PRIDE rally, they are moving toward making statements about the importance of new ways of relating to one another. Those who participate in the rally are working together toward liberation and healing for women in lesbian partnerships. The PRIDE march is not just another event that Helen and Beth can decide to attend or not; rather, it marks an important moment of decision for Beth and Helen as their participation sends signals and messages to others.

Working with Beth and Helen means inviting them to explore the depth of their covenantal partnership. Nurturing their partnership to develop around the qualities of love, justice, and mutuality offers Helen and Beth a way of framing their covenant with each other. Finding ways for them to negotiate through this conflict can invite them to move through another season in their relationship. Given what is known about Helen and Beth, it is probably safe to assume that they have entered into the season when conflict becomes more important as it defines the relationship in a new way. One critical piece of the caregiver's assessment with Beth and Helen is hearing the story of their partnership and its evolution. The current conflict can become part of a larger context as the caregiver celebrates other significant events in their relationship with them.

How Helen and Beth understand justice and the power dynamics in their relationship can offer insight into the nature of their covenant. Because women often come together in social places not defined by economic or class contingencies, it is not uncommon for lesbian partnerships to consist of two women from very different socioeconomic backgrounds. This can create serious imbalances of power. A pastoral caregiver will want to explore these issues with Beth and Helen since Beth's economic level is lower than Helen's. Discerning how that difference impacts the nature of the power of their relationship can assist them in finding mutual and just ways to make decisions in the midst of conflict.

Finally, a pastoral caregiver can be of tremendous help to Helen and Beth as they make their way through the maze of choices about coming out. There are very simple things a care specialist can do, such as role-playing with Beth or Helen what it might be like if Helen were to disclose her sexual identity to her children. The more someone can identify what she is most afraid of in coming out, the easier it is for her to assess whether she wants to take the risk involved in being open.

Since there is not one right way to move through the process of coming out, it is imperative that the pastoral caregiver provide a safe place for Beth and Helen to explore all of their fears and concerns. This process may take time. Helen should not participate in the march just because Beth wants to, and Beth should not decide that Helen will never be out of the closet just because she chooses not to participate in this year's event. There will be other opportunities when Helen may make different choices. Pastoral caregivers need to walk the longer journey with Helen and Beth if possible, inviting them to return to counseling whenever they are struggling with decisions about coming out. Issues of grief, pain, hurt, rejection, hope, transformation, and acceptance will, undoubtedly, be part of the longer journey of coming out.

Pastoral Theology
and Community

*Sara is the executive director of a relatively new pastoral counseling cen-
ter in a midsized city. She has been at the center for about eighteen
months and works with a board of directors made up of representatives
of various churches in town. This is one of the few ecumenical ventures
in town, and Sara has worked hard to make sure that the board reflects
different theological positions. Sara belongs to the United Church of
Christ and attends a local congregation that describes itself as moderate.
Other members of the board represent congregations from the following
traditions: American Baptist, National Baptist, Episcopalian, Lutheran
(E.L.C.A.), Presbyterian (U.S.A.), Roman Catholic, Unitarian, and United
Methodist. Up to this point the board has functioned well, agreeing on
such things as a mission statement, hiring policies, and general financial
matters.*

*The board meeting this past week focused on how to advertise the ser-
vices of the pastoral counseling center within the broader community.
Most referrals have come from the congregations that directly support the
center. Now, however, the board has decided that if it wants the center
to grow, it needs to reach out to the community in new ways. After several ideas surfaced, Paul, a member from a Presbyterian congregation,
suggested that the center advertise its services in the community lesbian
and gay newsletter. Paul noted that there were only a few affirmative
counseling resources available for lesbians, gay men, or bisexuals in the
community, and none of the one or two therapists who advertised currently in the newsletter identified themselves as pastoral counselors. This
initiated a conversation between Paul and Jim, the chair of the finance
committee. Jim, a member of a Lutheran community, was adamant that
the center not advertise unless it was clear about its position on homosexuality. From there the conversation spun into a debate about how
the churches in town would perceive their marketing efforts. If Sara and*

others in the counseling center actively recruited clients from the lesbian and gay community, some board members feared the center would lose financial support from local congregations. The majority of board members thought it would be all right if persons found their way to the counseling center through clergy referrals, but felt that advertising in the lesbian and gay newsletter was inviting trouble.

Finally the board agreed to talk to members of the congregations they represented. The next week Sara received many phone calls from persons in local churches, some of whom challenged Sara to counsel lesbians and gay men only if she would encourage them to seek heterosexual relationships. Others were more interested in protecting the center from sending the "wrong kind of message" by advertising in the newsletter. A few were family members of lesbians and gay men who wanted to know if they could come and talk to her about their concerns. Several of the phone calls mentioned withdrawing financial support if Sara and the board pursued advertising in the newsletter.

As Sara prepared for the board meeting the following week she wondered how to measure the costs and the benefits of advertising in the newsletter. Personally she welcomed clients who were lesbian and gay, but she was concerned about what the advertising would do to the financial status of this relatively new pastoral counseling center. Added to this was the center's burden of being the first ecumenical venture within the city that actually seemed to be working. Would it be worth upsetting the established ecumenical balance by raising the issue of homosexuality? Would it be possible to navigate through the various theological positions without persons losing respect for one another? The strongest voices seemed to be those who were opposed to the advertising. What did this debate mean for her, for the center, for the churches, and for the community in which she lives?

Sara's story reminds pastoral care specialists that conversations about homosexuality in the context of the church and its ministries can be explosive. This scenario clearly raises the issues of this book in a way that reflects the inner turmoil of many pastoral care specialists. How far can pastoral caregivers go in being proactive in their outreach to the lesbian community without encountering overwhelming controversy? What are the costs of being publicly supportive and affirmative of lesbians, gay men and bisexuals? Are the benefits worth the pain of fractured ecumenical relationships or lost dreams? This chapter does not attempt to answer all the questions apparent in this case. Instead, what is offered here is a conceptual framework for thinking about what it means to be involved in proactive pastoral care. Illustrative in this story are the struggles of many pastoral caregivers who genuinely want to serve lesbian parishioners and clients but who fear that the risks of being proactive may be greater than the ensuing benefits.

Three issues are addressed as we move toward the broader framework of pastoral theology, care, and counseling. First, the case study illuminates how various communities intersect on issues related to lesbian partnerships and pastoral care. Communal discourse and conversation are significant for lesbian partnerships and for pastoral care specialists. Second, the experiences of women who love women can assist in the construction of pastoral theological perspectives for such communal discourse. Theological themes, when approached with particular attention given to insights gained from working with women in lesbian relationships, are transformed in significant ways. Finally, this chapter invites pastoral care specialists to be proactive in addressing the needs of women in lesbian partnerships. Maintaining a proactive stance requires that caregivers evaluate their own internal homophobia as well as continue to work with passion and compassion to eradicate the injustice of heterosexism.

The Significance of Community

Several theological themes have surfaced in the previous discussions about pastoral care with women in lesbian partnerships. The theme of community is one which brings pastoral caregivers, women in lesbian partnerships, churches, and denominations together in a unique way. The words *community* and *covenant* have connections, according to J. Russell Burck, who notes: "*Community* is similar to *covenant*, which suggests an overcoming of barriers between strangers and an identifying of ways in which they can be resources for each other (to love one another)."[1] Communities are bound together by common values, interests, and concerns. They are not entities in which everyone agrees or all persons interpret things from the same perspective. Instead, communities are places where persons acknowledge differences while simultaneously strengthening the ties that bind them one to another. It seems appropriate to conclude a book on covenantal partnerships with considerations about what it means to be involved in communities at various levels. Most significantly, the barriers currently experienced between the communities of women who love women and the communities within faith traditions are to be challenged.

Lesbians and pastoral caregivers participate in communities that are often separate but may overlap in significant ways. An examination of each of the distinct kinds of communities in which women who love women and pastoral care specialists operate provides the opportunity to note stronger places of connection than immediately may be apparent. Together women in lesbian relationships and pastoral care specialists can create opportunities for discourse among diverse communities. Conversations between lesbians and pastoral care specialists can result in the building of communal covenants of love, justice, and mutuality, confronting the building of barriers that keep one another strangers.

Women in lesbian relationships share the fact that they are primarily involved with other women. However, the diversity of this community should not be underestimated. While this book has attempted to illustrate some of the richness of this community through the use of case studies, these stories do not completely reflect the diversity to be found in lesbian communities. Women in lesbian partnerships cross the boundaries of age, class, race, religious background, and political affiliation. They may not agree with one another about everything and they may not enjoy one another all the time, but they ultimately respect and support one another's lesbian relationships and the right of women to love women. Thus, diverse groups of women are brought together because of their primary emotional, physical, and sexual affections for women.

Women who love women intersect with other communities, including communities where they are unwelcomed or unwanted. Many women hesitate to be open in the communities where they live for fear that they will face discrimination, harassment, or bias. Feeling uncomfortable walking hand in hand with their partners in public does not reflect an uneasiness with their orientation identity but reflects concretely the reality that they are often treated as strangers in those communities. Some lesbians develop a posture of watching over their shoulders to see who is observing them. This should not be interpreted as paranoia, but as a way of protecting themselves in the world.

Safety is a significant issue for women in lesbian relationships. The rise in attacks aimed at homosexuals, particularly against the gay men's community, has an emotional affect on women who love women. Recognizing that there are persons in the community around them who want to physically harm them because of their orientation can drive women deeper into their closets or radicalize them so they become strong political activists. Safety, however, is not limited to concerns for their living spaces. Emotional insecurity is experienced by women who fear rejection from their families of origin because of the women they choose to love. Job uncertainty arises as women acknowledge that their careers may be lost, or at least suffer, if their peers, colleagues, or bosses discover their lesbian identities.

The very real need for safety affects women in various ways. Some women become more fearful as they recognize that they have much to lose in being self-identified lesbians. Wanting places where they can experience being comfortable and feeling at home, women sometimes seek community in enclaves designated as lesbian- or gay-friendly. Many larger cities have particular areas where many lesbians live, serving as a community of choice for women in lesbian partnerships. Other women seek support in social settings such as women's bookstores, women-identified gathering places, or coffeehouses. Places where women can meet one another, greet one another with a hug, and hold hands if they so choose, offer safety as women gather the internal strength they need to face a world that is sometimes hostile, often ambivalent, and rarely open and affirming. In these sanctuaries women talk openly about their lives, share with one another their celebrations and their losses, and participate in communities that accept them and their relationships.

Unfortunately, churches and communities of faith are identified as some of the most unwelcoming places for women in lesbian relationships. The painful stories reported by women who have been told they were evil or sinful because they love other women serve to remind lesbians that they must walk carefully in local churches. For this reason women often do not turn to pastoral caregivers or others who represent the church in their search for safety. Communities of faith are filled with women who endure by living double lives. In public they are lay leaders or clergy while in other arenas they are lesbians who keep one of the most important aspects of their lives in the closet. It is not safe for these women to be open in their local churches and denominations.

Since institutional churches are not usually viewed as sanctuaries for women partners, lesbians yearn for other communities where they can nurture their spiritual lives, affirm their faiths, and celebrate their relationships.[2] Welcoming fellowships are found in the Metropolitan Community Church or in congregations that intentionally identify themselves as open and affirming of lesbians and gay men. Often, however, these local communities of faith take stands that are viewed as being outside the official jurisdiction of the denomination. For example, the Reconciling Congregation movement within the United Methodist denomination is not endorsed by the governing body of that church. The prophetic voices of the handful of open churches are not always welcomed in the public domain of denominational discourse.

Because few congregations make public their open and affirming stances, lesbians and gay men create their own spiritual communities at the margins of their denominations. Dan Spencer notes the importance of claiming a "church at the margins," one which affirms the wholeness of lesbians and gay men. He suggests that the task of community is not merely to minister *to* the margins of a community, but to *make the margins themselves a community:*

> The *ecclesia* of lesbians and gay men will be a *community at the margins:* of the society, the broader church, our communities and families of origin.

Gay men and lesbians typically find ourselves at the margins of whatever other community we belong to, whether these communities are shaped by racial or ethnic identity, by class location, or by religious affiliation. Claiming the particularity of our identity as lesbian or gay usually cuts us off from our communities of origin, which might otherwise serve as liberating sources in our struggles. We cannot simply return to our roots for sources of liberation, but must forge new sources from the communities we create.[3]

Communities at the margins become places where women in lesbian partnerships find belonging, affirmation, and support for their spiritual, emotional, sexual, and relational lives.

Lesbians, gay men and bisexuals find liberation and empowerment in these communities at the margins. Instead of spending their energies fighting for safety within the structures of the institutional church, the communities at the margins become intentional sanctuaries for spiritual growth. Lesbians do not always participate in local churches and communities of faith where they can challenge, inform, and shape the theology and ministries of the global church. This is a significant loss for the church, and a loss that denominations and churches do not always recognize. The church is less than whole because of the absence of many lesbians, gay men, and bisexuals.

Lesbians create communities of choice. Sometimes they are underground and covert, with women accessing information about the "community" only through conversations with other lesbians. At other times communities are open and visible as they work for justice in more public arenas. Pastoral representatives of the church must not deny the ability of lesbian communities to offer sanctuary to women who have not experienced such safety in local communities of faith. Pastoral care specialists who are intentional about working with lesbians should be aware of the coffeehouses, bookstores, spirituality groups, and gathering places that serve lesbian communities. These communities are significant to pastoral care with women in lesbian relationships since lesbian-affirming places offer a welcome to women partners in ways that churches have not been able to extend.

Pastoral caregivers are also part of numerous connecting communities. Primarily, pastoral representatives participate in their respective communities of faith, denominational judicatories, and ecclesiastical bodies. Caregivers cannot escape the responsibility of having both priestly and prophetic voices within those communities. To deny either the priestly or the prophetic role is to deny the fullness of the call to be pastoral caregivers. Representing congregations and denominations as pastoral leaders requires that pastoral caregivers engage in communal discourse with churches as they discern what it means to care with women in lesbian relationships.

Being prophets within churches is often understood as a secondary function by pastoral care specialists who do the majority of their work through the offering of counseling services. However, not to be part of the broader church networks that promote open and affirmative care for all persons, including lesbian partners, is a denial of the comprehensive call to embracing a pastoral perspective.

Pastoral care specialists also participate in communities of other professionals. Pastoral representatives intersect with those who are mental health professionals, hospital personnel, or others who are considered to be colleagues and peers. In those contexts pastoral caregivers convey the perspectives of pastoral theology and the commitments of their particular faith traditions. Even though specific conversations may be shaped by the perspectives of mental health providers, pastoral caregivers can offer insight and leadership by their presence in these communities of professionals as they challenge other professionals to offer genuine and careful counseling with women who love women. By connecting with other professionals, pastoral care specialists can use their voices to engage colleagues in communal discourse.

Third, the towns and cities where pastoral care specialists live and work are places for engaging in communal discourse. These are often the same neighborhoods in which lesbians feel unwelcome or unsafe. Being proactive in these communities means leading educational efforts, raising the concerns of lesbian partnerships in public places, and working toward liberation on behalf of the communities at the margins. Usually pastoral care specialists in these communities have a stronger voice than do persons on the margins. Integral to a communal perspective of pastoral theology, care, and counseling is the use of that voice to break silences in the dominant culture and to talk openly about the concerns of women in lesbian relationships.

Pastoral caregivers should provide some of the connections between congregations, denominations, cities, towns, and the communities at the margins. Specialists often find it too easy to wait until someone presents an issue in counseling before they seek resources in the community. This book assumes that pastoral care specialists want to be proactive in meeting those at the margins, not simply waiting for women to appear in their offices for care and counseling but actively initiating conversations with lesbian-affirming organizations. One way to provide the link between churches and communities of lesbian women is to become familiar with groups such as Parents and Friends of Lesbians and Gays (PFLAG), Affirmation, Integrity, or other unofficial denominational support and advocacy groups for lesbians, gay men, and bisexuals. Pastoral caregivers can volunteer to give lectures, offer support groups for families, or teach adult education courses in local churches as ways of engaging the various communities in discourse with one another.

Community is an important theological theme. Pastoral care specialists who are willing to become leaders in communal discourse are those who actively seek to know the community at the margins. The vast majority of pastoral caregivers are familiar with the communities of faith with which they work, but it takes added effort to connect to communities where they are less well known. Caregivers serve to interpret one community to another and to make the connections visible between communities. This task of becoming a link between communities of faith and communities at the margins is essential in offering pastoral care that is community based. Pastoral representatives break down the barriers that keep people strangers to one another, building instead a communion where persons come to know one another with love, justice, and mutuality.

Constructive Pastoral Theology

Reflections arising from the praxis of care with women in lesbian relationships offer new directions for pastoral theology. One aspect of pastoral theology is highlighted as caregivers reflect theologically about the nature of their work, about what it means to be human, and about how to convey messages of hope and good news to those who come to them for care. A second aspect of pastoral theology is the use of insights gleaned from praxis to challenge and reform theological understandings when they seem to be lacking or failing to match the particularities of persons' experience. Pastoral caregivers inform theology as they reflect upon the stories, the experiences, and the lives of women in lesbian partnerships. Various theological themes, many having been briefly touched upon in this book, arise in the context of caring with women who love women. Theology includes such diverse subjects as what it means to be the church, questions of moral stances and positions, interpretations of biblical stories, the development of covenants and partnerships, and the connections between spirituality and sexuality.

Pastoral caregivers accept constructing pastoral theological perspectives as part of their task. Those who hear the stories of lesbian partnerships ought to feel compelled to participate in the ongoing construction of a pastoral theology that is informed by these stories. Narratives from the lives of women who love women are brought together with narratives of faith to create new meaning in the lives of persons. The community of those who call themselves pastoral theologians will continue to be graced by reflecting upon the stories they hear. Three areas, in particular, might be shaped by ongoing pastoral theological reflection with lesbian partners.

First, pastoral theology can learn from the experiences of women in lesbian partnerships by reflecting upon the significance of rituals and symbols. Persons within churches and within lesbian communities have worked diligently to create meaningful ritual moments. Some of these sacred events are intended to add sanctity to lesbian partnerships that are in the process of being formed and shaped.[4] Other ritual moments occur as women change the nature of their previous covenants, moving away from particular partnerships but pledging to remain steadfast in their friendships. Sacred events could also be developed for women who bring children into their lesbian families and invite their communities of faith to participate in the blessing and raising of those children.

It might seem simple to take the current rituals and symbols of the church and make them fit the experiences of women in lesbian partnerships. But women who love women bring distinctive theological perspectives and assumptions to what it means to be in relationship with one another. Hence, continued reflection upon the differences between being married in the traditional sense and creating new kinds of covenants between women can lead to constructing new pastoral theological perspectives. Communal discourse occurs as women in lesbian partnerships are met by pastoral caregivers who can help them reflect on the significant events in their lives and create ritual moments. Pastoral caregivers who, in turn, theologically reflect with family members of lesbians and with churches and denominations about what it means to participate in such ritual moments with women partners, offer various communities the opportunity to be in meaningful conversation with one another.

A second issue within the lesbian community that can contribute to pastoral theology is that of silence and its connection to liberation. The language and metaphor of closets and coming out illuminates the difference between being silenced and choosing to be silent. Many women do not feel that they have a choice about being silent, experiencing the silence as something imposed upon them by their churches and their culture. Those who wonder why women have to talk about their sexuality or "flaunt it in public" do not understand how those comments encourage people to remain silent about their intimate and significant relationships. Such imposed silence prevents genuine freedom and liberation. Silence becomes a theological issue as women reflect upon the power of their voices to speak the truth about their lives and their covenants. When silence is imposed from the outside, it is difficult to hear the voice of God on the inside.

Many churches and pastoral caregivers have chosen to be silent rather than to confront the painful issues and emotions that often surface in conversations about homosexuality. In the process, churches have perpetuated the oppression of those women who have more to lose by speaking up and whose voices are not always heard when they choose to speak. Women who love women challenge the church to give up the silence about the injustices perpetrated against women in lesbian relationships. Pastoral representatives have a place within their churches from which they can speak and be heard. Specialists who theologically reflect with congregations and communities of faith about what it means to impose silence on others are encouraging communal discourse as they seek liberation in the lives of lesbians, in their families, in their churches, and in their communities.

A third and broader area for pastoral theology is reflection on what it means to be a community of faith. In traditional language this is often talked about as ecclesiology, or the purpose and nature of the church. The church, as embodied in local congregations and ecclesial structures, is challenged by women in lesbian partnerships who attempt to relate meaningfully within mainline denominations. Yet many churches have structured their faith commitments in ways that serve to actively discourage the spiritual, emotional, and relational lives of women who love women. When women who yearn to be connected to God, self, and others in appropriate and faithful ways are rejected from having a significant place within communities of faith, the church needs to reexamine its call and purpose.

This relates, of course, to a proactive position held by those who share in the leadership of the church. Faithful pastoral caregivers struggle to respond to their inner call to be present with women in lesbian partnerships, but feel a need to protect themselves from controversy by avoiding visible and vocal public and communal discourse. Perhaps the question with which pastoral counselors must continue to struggle is how to be more than simply a mental health alternative in a church that needs to be challenged anew by the gospel. Being pastoral inevitably means being connected to ecclesial structures in such a way that the risks of being open and affirming will be met by a community of people who desperately wish to embody the call to be the church in the world. Pastoral care specialists who take leadership in the task of challenging the church should not feel that they are standing alone in the community of faith.

Pastoral theology should continue to search for new metaphors and theological images that honor and respect the journeys taken by women in lesbian partnerships. Searching for biblical stories, theological insights, and compassionate ways of caring for women creates new opportunities for theological reflection within the context of communities of faith.

Proactive Pastoral Care Specialists

Proactive pastoral care specialists are women and men who not only are willing to respond to women who come to them for care and counseling but also intentionally create safe places for women, their families, and their churches. Two things are required of pastoral caregivers who wish to create sanctuaries where persons can address the complex issues raised in this book. First, caregivers should work on their own issues of homophobia, being honest about times when they need to refer their lesbian or gay parishioners and clients to other persons. Second, pastoral care specialists should combine their passion for justice with their compassion for human beings by working to eradicate structures of heterosexism.

Self-evaluation and the Pastoral Care Specialist

Heterosexism and homophobia operate at the unconscious level for most pastoral caregivers. Given that these dynamics are part of the culture in which most people grow up, it is common for caregivers to carry the residual effects of bias and prejudice into their practices and their belief systems. Recognizing external structures of injustice is made more difficult by the presence of internalized homophobia in pastoral caregivers.

Internalized homophobia refers to feelings of anger or rejection toward lesbians, gay men, or bisexuals. Parallel to these feelings are internal fears of being attracted to persons of the same sex, being attractive to someone of the same sex, or being perceived by others as homosexual. The feelings are internalized in such a way that they often work at a deeply unconscious and subliminal level. As a result, pastoral care specialists who want to offer the most appropriate and genuine care to women in lesbian partnerships must work conscientiously to discover the biases, prejudices, or internal fears that they carry into their praxis. In discovering these internalizations, pastoral caregivers can then approach women with greater care and integrity.

Common to the therapeutic training and experience of most pastoral caregivers is an assessment of transference and countertransference. While the issues of homophobia are directly related to the dynamics of transferential material, internalized homophobia is a little different. Most training programs carefully examine the bases for anxieties and feelings raised within the pastoral caregiver by their parishioners and clients. Relatively less energy is spent thinking about how sociocultural biases or prejudices become incorporated into the internal structures of caregivers. Homophobia is a common dynamic in a world that actively discriminates against women in lesbian relationships. It is present in therapists, counselors, clinicians, pastors, and even in women who love women. Lesbian partners carry internalized homophobia as they worry about how pastoral caregivers will respond to their life stories or their relationships.

Pastoral care specialists who learn to recognize internalized homophobia in themselves will be more open to lesbians and more aware of the dynamics of the partners with whom they are working. Without this self-evaluation, internal feelings and reactions of the caregivers themselves may receive more attention than the concerns of their parishioners and clients. In order to recognize internalized homophobia pastoral caregivers must reckon with their souls and search to understand the feelings they experience when working with women who love women or with gay men. Not attending to the dynamics of internalized homophobia can result in caregivers who inadvertently perpetuate systems of injustice rather than being vessels of graceful care. Essentially this means that women in lesbian relationships need pastoral caregivers who have intentionally struggled with their own sexuality to insure that the care offered reflects genuine concern rather than insecure feelings.

One aspect of recognizing internalized homophobia involves attending to the comfort level of caregivers as they work with women in lesbian relationships. Self-evaluative exercises can help pastoral care specialists identify those places where they may need to examine their feelings. For example, going to a bookstore and browsing in the homosexual literature section often raises feelings. Keeping track of the fears, the concerns, or the anxieties that arise internally can illuminate one's own homophobia. For instance, does looking at the books on lesbian sex provoke anxiety about who might be watching? The caregiver might attend a lesbian or gay event or a service at the local Metropolitan Community Church and pay attention to feelings as they emerge. Is it comfortable to be with women who are holding other women's hands or with men who are hugging one another? What is it like to have others assume that you are lesbian or gay just because you are at this event?

A less intimidating activity is to spend more time with persons of one's own gender and explore the feelings that arise with these friends or colleagues. What is it like to be emotionally connected with others of the same sex? Is it comfortable to share intimately in conversations with other men or other women? A more proactive exercise is to volunteer to speak to a local church group about homosexuality. Take an extremely affirmative stance or write the first draft of the speech with the assumption that only supportive statements will be made about lesbians and their partnerships. Identify any discomfort in imagining how other persons might respond to these statements, particularly those who might deeply disagree with this perspective.

Pastoral care specialists who work with women partners should be comfortable with their own feelings about lesbian relationships. This comfort makes it possible to listen more attentively, be more responsive in offering care, and remain more open to those who disagree with one's own theoretical or moral perspectives on homosexuality.

As pastoral caregivers examine their internalized homophobia and its negative effect upon their counseling, they consciously adopt stronger lesbian-affirmative approaches in their work with women in lesbian relationships. Kristine Falco notes the importance of such approaches in her four categories of responses typical of therapists: "The You're Not a Lesbian Response," "The Lecture" (often from a religious or developmental arrest theory), "The Liberal Response" (lesbians are the same as heterosexuals), and "The Inadequate Response" (where talk about the client's lesbianism is avoided).[5] None of these responses is particularly helpful for women in lesbian relationships. They vary from denial of the relationships to a benign refusal to recognize the distinctiveness of women who love women. In a similar vein, pastoral caregivers who are merely tolerant of lesbians are not genuinely helpful to their parishioners or clients. Women partners need care specialists who are proactive in their acceptance and who are not afraid of their orientation.

Not every pastoral caregiver should work with women in lesbian relationships. Those specialists who are uncomfortable with their own sexuality or who are uneasy being with women who share their affection and love with other women ought to refer their parishioners and clients to other caregivers. Similarly, those persons who have not discerned where they stand in terms of the moral perspectives they bring to their work with women in lesbian relationships should probably find other community resources for women partners. Ambivalence and ambiguity on the part of the caregiver serve as barriers to genuine pastoral response.

A growing body of literature suggests that lesbian women ought to be seen by lesbian therapists who publicly affirm their own orientations. The argument is based upon the belief that lesbians can move more quickly into doing their own work when they worry less about attitudes of latent heterosexuality or homophobia in the caregivers. Being affirmed by lesbian therapists who understand themselves to be healthy and whole can add significant power to women in lesbian relationships.[6] This raises an interesting concern for pastoral counselors who are not lesbians. If it is better for lesbians to see therapists who self-identify as lesbians, how helpful can straight men and women be as pastoral care specialists? Should the latter always refer to lesbian therapists?

For some lesbian partners it may be important to see a lesbian therapist. This need should not be interpreted as a resistance or avoidance of pastoral care or counseling. Instead, it may be a healthy and appropriate example of self-care and self-direction. Most often, women who need to be seen by lesbian therapists are those who have experienced intense hurt or rejection in the church and who find themselves unable to trust pastoral caregivers for a variety of reasons. Women who experience not only the heterosexism of the church but also its sexism may need to work with lesbian therapists. Other lesbian partners are helped immensely when they use the services of lesbian therapists during particular periods in their lives. For example, some women who are moving toward self-identification as lesbians may find working with lesbian therapists to be extremely affirming as they take their next steps in the process. Seeing a lesbian professional can add internal strength to the life of the parishioner or client.

Important dynamics surface for those pastoral counselors who are lesbian in their orientation and who work with women partnerships. Depending upon whether pastoral caregivers self-identify as lesbians or whether they are in the closet in their denominational structures, women partnerships may raise the anxiety level of the caregiver. This is not necessarily to be understood as something negative for the recipient of the care. Often women who have not self-identified as lesbian in a public way but who are private about their lesbian lives can intuitively understand the intense dynamics of issues that women in lesbian relationships have to face. A question with which many lesbian pastoral care specialists struggle is that of "coming out" with their clients. Discerning when and how to be open and honest as a lesbian pastoral caregiver is an issue that should be broached within a broader supportive community. Those pastoral representatives who are lesbian or gay have much to lose and to gain from such openness.

For many women in lesbian relationships, however, pastoral caregivers who express openness, honesty, and affirmation can be helpful. At times women may turn to pastoral representatives because they want to work on their faith journeys or on their spiritual lives. Pastoral care specialists can be particularly helpful to women who are in the process of exploring their self-identification as lesbians in their communities of faith. Women often turn to pastoral caregivers in their roles as representatives of churches for help in understanding scripture, dealing with families of origin who are raising moral questions, or investigating images of God that support and affirm lesbian identities.

Adequate training, careful supervision, and strong support in the lesbian community for pastoral caregivers who are lesbians can provide what is needed for giving appropriate care to parishioners and clients. Lesbian pastoral caregivers face the common experience of being in social situations within the lesbian community where clients are present. Such caregivers must clearly state the boundaries of the relationship, with the assumption that caregivers and clients will see one another in the lesbian community because of its limited size.

Pastoral care specialists who have assessed their internalized homophobia and who are comfortable with their sexuality can be of tremendous assistance to women in lesbian relationships. As in all situations, pastoral caregivers who are honest, forthright, and clear about their own perspectives provide the best care for women partnerships.

Passion and Compassion

Passions reflect intense convictions about particular ideas, positions, or beliefs. People are energized in their spiritual lives, producing vitality and depth, as they commit themselves to those things they hold most valuable and important. Pastoral caregivers have not always been known for being passionate about issues of justice. Working with women in lesbian relationships should result in pastoral care specialists who become passionate about eradicating those systemic injustices that prevent women from experiencing increased freedom and liberation in their relationships with one another. Work within the pastoral care office cannot be separated from prophetic movements toward liberation and justice that affect the lives of those who seek out care and counsel.

Pastoral care specialists are often thought of as compassionate women and men. Listening to stories of pain and hurt, trauma and despair, fear and rejection leads to increased sensitivity and empathy. In their work with women in lesbian relationships pastoral caregivers offer sacred spaces for women to share their vulnerabilities and their hopes. Most often it is a compassionate nature that draws a pastoral caregiver into this kind of ministry.

Proactive pastoral care specialists integrate their passion for justice with their compassion for human beings. In so doing they are convinced of the need for justice and liberation for all, including those within the communities at the margins. However, their passion is tempered with the compassion of knowing that issues of moral complexity elicit deep and perplexing feelings. Without compassion, proactive pastoral caregivers might work to eradicate heterosexism without being aware that even changes for justice can create chaos, confusion, and pain in human beings. Without passion, pastoral care specialists might respond only to the hurt and despair in individual lives and not move beyond the counseling office to actively change structures that contribute to the pain of human beings. Passion without compassion becomes abrasive and lacks genuine empathy for others. Compassion without passion becomes sentimental care that lacks depth and integrity.

Pastoral representatives become prophetic priests who minister not only to those who come for care and counsel but also to the broader communities in which they live. Being proactive as pastoral care specialists means engaging local churches and denominations in serious reflection about the structures of heterosexism that support active discrimination against women in lesbian partnerships. If pastoral counselors are to be trusted to offer sacred spaces to those they counsel, they must also move outside the confines of their offices to engage those within the lesbian community. Similarly, pastoral caregivers need to take leadership in churches that honestly want to struggle with the issues of homosexuality. Becoming a spokesperson for proactive stances on behalf of lesbians does not mean speaking *for* women who love women. Instead, being proactive means joining *with* the lesbian community in calling the church to accountability for its lack of inclusiveness.

Taking a proactive stance does represent potential loss for pastoral caregivers who do not want to be uncomfortable or to rock the boat. For some pastoral counselors, being proactive may mean turning down referrals from churches that are interested only in perpetuating heterosexism by demanding that counselors approach women in lesbian relationships from the perspective of encouraging them to repent of their sins. Other pastoral care-givers experience anxiety as they move into areas where they have previously not worked. It does take more energy to join communities at the margins.

Challenging heterosexism means challenging communities of faith and churches to work toward love, justice, and mutuality in their covenantal re-lationships with one another. The building up of community requires that the same qualities that are encouraged for covenantal lesbian partnerships be embraced in communities that have previously understood lesbians to be strangers.

A Proactive
Pastoral Counseling Center

In the case history at the beginning of this chapter Sara and the board of the pastoral counseling center represent the dynamic tensions present when the concerns of women in lesbian relationships intersect with those of communities of faith. The anxieties expressed by those on the board are common to many faithful persons who struggle to be both passionate and compassionate in their ministries. Thinking about this case from the per-spective of the various communities identified in this chapter illustrates how the pastoral counseling center might take a proactive stance within this community.

First, Sara, the staff of the pastoral counseling center, and the members of the board are participants in various congregations. Together they rep-resent the diversity and breadth of moral perspectives lifted up in the first chapter of this book. Individuals and families within the congregations that the board represents probably experience the range of feelings about and responses to homosexuality. One positive decision taken by the board at its meeting was to return to the respective local congregations to talk with others about the concerns of the board. This action invited people to con-front the issue and talk about what it means to be in ministry with those in the lesbian community. One person raising the concern led to opportuni-ties for the center to participate in communal discourse.

In this case the pastoral counseling center might well take the initiative to offer educational opportunities for congregations and individuals who want to explore the issues related to homosexuality. The center could pro-vide space in the building along with facilitators (the pastoral counselors in the center) to attend to both the emotional and cognitive levels of the con-versation. Such an event gives people an opportunity to express their thoughts, their fears, and their perspectives. In offering an educational ex-perience the staff members of the counseling center bring their pastoral theological resources to the congregations they serve.

The counseling center must move beyond the realm of individual com-passion. In so doing, it takes seriously its role within the communities of faith represented by those who contribute financing to the center. The need for the pastoral counseling center to respond to the churches with concrete opportunities to talk about what it means to be passionate about seeking justice can engage congregations in communal discourse with one another and with the lesbian communities at the margins.

The pastoral counseling center is also connected to a broader group of mental health professionals. Certainly Sara and her colleagues are in con-versations with others in the community who provide mental health ser-vices. To be proactive Sara could take the initiative on behalf of the center to offer a workshop on homophobia, heterosexism, and counseling. Self-education about the concerns women in lesbian relationships bring to pas-toral counselors can only produce a higher quality of care. Many excellent resources that speak to these concerns are available. Reading together some of the resource materials mentioned in this book can provide an in-tellectual environment for professionals to gather and discuss their con-cerns and perspectives. By doing this Sara would connect the pastoral counseling center to the concerns of the professionals with whom she works as peers and colleagues. At the same time offering this event would send messages to those professionals that Sara and the pastoral counseling center are concerned about these issues and are interested in working care-fully with women in lesbian relationships.

Third, Sara, the pastoral counseling staff, and the members of the board live in a community where there are most certainly lesbians, gay men, and bisexuals. As members of this broader community Sara and her colleagues must determine whom they will see and when they will take special initia-tive to seek clients and referrals. Pastoral counseling centers make decisions every day about who it is in their best interest to serve. Sometimes these de-cisions are made on financial grounds, while at other times they are made on the bases of geographical locations. Questions about who will be served by this particular pastoral counseling center must be placed in tension with questions about why particular target groups for service are chosen.

The benefits of serving the under-served or those who live in the com-munities at the margins are at least threefold. First, working with commu-nities at the margins broadens the base of pastoral theology. Persons on the edges have much to teach those in the mainstream. To not take the initia-tive necessary to let persons in communities at the margins know that they are welcomed and affirmed in this pastoral counseling center means to lose the opportunity to be informed theologically by their experiences.

Second, working with women in lesbian partnerships means standing in solidarity with people who are oppressed. As pastoral counseling centers explore what it means to be caregivers using traditional counseling mod-els, they are continually confronted with the fact that they do not often stand in solidarity with the poor, the oppressed, or the under-served. The benefit of being proactive for the pastoral counseling center is that it will more adequately embrace a fuller understanding of what it means to be a community of faith.

A third benefit of being proactive in initiating conversations with women in lesbian relationships is that those communities often are in search of pastoral representatives who can bring theological resources to their lives. As such, once the word is out that this counseling center actively encourages women in lesbian partnerships to enter their doors, the counseling center's visibility within the broader community will be raised. Not only women in lesbian relationships but also their families of origin, their families of choice, and others will be encouraged to seek the pastoral care services of this counseling center.

The pastoral counseling center can connect the various communities through educational opportunities, counseling programs, groups for families, or partnership retreats for women in relationships. Sara, the board, and the pastoral counseling center stand at the precipice of deciding whether to be silent or to speak out. They probably can afford to be silent in terms of their financial status. However, being silent compromises their integrity as pastoral representatives within the other communities in which they live. The question is not whether they can financially afford to speak up; rather, the question is whether they can spiritually afford to be silent.

Conclusion

In this book I have taken seriously the gifts and graces lesbian partners have to offer the church, local congregations, and the field of pastoral theology and care. At the same time, I have attempted to struggle honestly with concrete issues that most often bring women into the office of the pastoral caregiver. It is apparent that as pastoral care specialists we must continue to learn from the lives of others and challenge the more negative perceptions of what it means to be women who love women. Many women and men welcome the presence of pastoral representatives who are not only affirmative in their stances but proactive in seeking justice in their communities of faith.

Being a proactive caregiver by celebrating and supporting lesbian relationships of love, justice, and mutuality is not without cost. Emotional, physical, and spiritual energies are required when confronting heterosexism and homophobia within ourselves, our communities of faith, and our culture. Yet commensurate with the costs are the gifts of increasing freedom, liberation, and goodness for lesbians, gay men, bisexuals, partners, families, and churches.

Notes

Chapter 1:
Pastoral Counseling
and Women in Lesbian Relationships

1. The case studies presented in this book are composites from diverse pastoral experiences with women in lesbian relationships. Any similarity to particular persons is coincidental.

2. Patricia Beattie Jung and Ralph F. Smith, *Heterosexism: An Ethical Challenge* (Albany: State University of New York Press), 21–31. Compare these positions to those outlined by Nelson, who suggests that there are four theological stances: rejecting-punitive, rejecting non-punitive, qualified acceptance, full acceptance. James B. Nelson, *Embodiment: An Approach to Sexuality and Christian Theology* (Minneapolis: Augsburg Publishing House, 1978), 188–99.

3. Jung and Smith, *Heterosexism*, 22.

4. Illustrative of this perspective are Irving Bieber, *Homosexuality: A Psychoanalytic Study* (Northvale, N.J.: Jason Aronson, 1988); Joseph Nocolosi, *Healing Homosexuality: Case Stories of Reparative Therapy* (Northvale, N.J.: Jason Aronson, 1993); and Charles W. Socarides, *Homosexuality: Psychoanalytic Therapy* (Northvale, N.J.: Jason Aronson, 1989).

5. Jung and Smith, *Heterosexism*, 24.

6. Ibid., 25–26.

7. Ibid., 24.

8. For an illustration of this, see John F. Harvey, O.S.F.S., *The Homosexual Person: New Thinking in Pastoral Care* (San Francisco: Ignatius Press, 1987).

9. Jung and Smith, *Heterosexism*, 26.

10. Some of the mainline denominational stances lean toward this perspective. Persons are affirmed in their sexuality but encouraged to be closeted or overly cautious about expressing their orientations.

11. Jung and Smith, *Heterosexism*, 27.

12. Ibid., 30.

13. Ibid., 30.

14. Some of the most helpful works are John Boswell, *Christianity, Social Tolerance, and Homosexuality* (Chicago: University of Chicago Press, 1980); Gary David Comstock, *Gay Theology without Apology* (Cleveland: Pilgrim Press, 1993); George R. Edwards, *Gay/Lesbian Liberation: A Biblical Perspective* (New York: Pilgrim Press, 1984); Victor Paul Furnish, *Moral Teaching of Paul* (Nashville: Abingdon Press, 1979); Jung and Smith, *Heterosexism*; John J. McNeill, *The Church and the Homosexual*, 3d ed. (Boston: Beacon Press,

1988); Letha Scanzoni and Virginia Ramey Mollenkott, *Is the Homosexual My Neighbor? Another Christian View* (San Francisco: Harper & Row, 1978); Robin Scroggs, *The New Testament and Homosexuality* (Philadelphia: Fortress Press, 1983); Phyllis Trible, *Texts of Terror* (Philadelphia: Fortress Press, 1984), 75.

15. For a helpful perspective on interpreting scripture from liberation themes, see Robert McAfee Brown, *Theology in a New Key: Responding to Liberation Themes* (Philadelphia: Westminster Press, 1978); Edwards, *Gay/Lesbian Liberation.*

16. Jung and Smith, *Heterosexism,* 62.

17. Edwards, *Gay/Lesbian Liberation,* 26.

18. Scroggs, *The New Testament and Homosexuality,* 140. See also Bernadette Brooten, "Paul's Views on the Nature of Women and Female Homoeroticism," in *Homosexuality and Religion and Philosophy,* ed. Wayne R. Dynes and Stephen Donaldson, 57–83 (New York: Garland Publishing, 1992).

19. The word *homosexuality* does not appear in the Hebrew or Greek scriptures. In scripture what is being alluded to most often is not "orientation" but particular "behavior." Whether the behavior described in the scripture can be appropriated to condemn same-sex relationships formed in the context of loving care is a matter of interpretation of scripture. Edwards, *Gay/Lesbian Liberation,* 14n27.

20. For an interesting interpretation of the David and Jonathon story, see T. Horner, *Jonathan Loved David: Homosexuality in Biblical Times* (Philadelphia: Westminster Press, 1978). While I do not agree with his perspective on this story, it does raise some interesting questions for the biblical interpreter.

21. See Joanne Carlson Brown and Carole R. Bohn, *Christianity, Patriarchy and Abuse: A Feminist Critique* (New York: Pilgrim Press, 1989); Carol P. Christ and Judith Plaskow, eds., *Womanspirit Rising: A Feminist Reader in Religion* (San Francisco: Harper & Row, 1979); Gerda Lerner, *The Creation of Patriarchy* (New York: Oxford University Press, 1986); Rosemary Radford Ruether, *Sexism and God-Talk: Toward a Feminist Theology* (Boston: Beacon Press, 1983).

22. See Valerie DeMarinis, *Critical Caring: A Feminist Model for Pastoral Psychology* (Louisville, Ky.: Westminster/John Knox Press, 1993); Maxine Glaz and Jeanne Stevenson Moessner, eds., *Women in Travail and Transition: A New Pastoral Care* (Minneapolis: Fortress Press, 1991); Carroll Saussy, *God Images and Self Esteem: Empowering Women in a Patriarchal Society* (Louisville, Ky.: Westminster/John Knox Press, 1991); James Poling, *The Abuse of Power: A Theological Problem* (Nashville: Abingdon Press, 1991).

23. Judith Worell and Pam Remer, *Feminist Perspectives in Therapy: An Empowerment Model for Women* (New York: John Wiley & Sons, 1992), 9.

24. Ibid., 13.

25. DeMarinis, *Critical Caring,* 18. In this context she notes three other elements of feminist theology and psychosocial theory which are helpful for pastoral counseling: (1) feminist positions "offer access to the wisdom coming from voices challenging existing perceptions across disciplines"; (2) they "understand belief systems and their influence to be an essential part of the way

human life and relationships come to have meaning"; and (3) "feminist theology and feminist psychosocial theory incorporate a praxis methodology, which demands that action and reflection work in tandem." DeMarinis, *Critical Caring*, 18. Added to the work of Worell and Remer in feminist psychotherapy are the following: Nancy Chodorow, *The Reproduction of Mothering: Psychoanalysis and the Sociology of Gender* (Berkeley: University of California Press, 1978); Luise Eichenbaum and Susie Orbach, *Understanding Women: A Feminist Psychoanalytic Approach* (New York: Basic Books, 1983); Jean Baker Miller, *Toward a New Psychology of Women* (Boston: Beacon Press, 1976); Marianne Walters, Betty Carter, Peggy Papp, and Olga Silverstein, *The Invisible Web: Gender Patterns in Family Relationships* (New York: Guilford Press, 1988).

26. Worell and Remer, *Feminist Perspectives in Therapy*, 91.

27. For a painful story about the power of destructive theological assertions, see DeMarinis, *Critical Caring*, 121–44.

28. Worell and Remer, *Feminist Perspectives in Therapy*, 94.

29. Mutuality is a major thesis in Carter Heyward's *Touching our Strength: The Erotic as Power and the Love of God* (San Francisco: Harper & Row, 1989). The qualities that she describes will become more central to conversations about covenant in chapter 3.

30. Worell and Remer, *Feminist Perspectives in Therapy*, 97.

31. For pastoral care specialists who would like to look more carefully at their own biases around issues of gender, Worell and Remer open each chapter with a self-assessment tool.

32. Two helpful explications of this are found in Beverly Wildung Harrison, "Misogyny and Homophobia: The Unexplored Connections," in *Making the Connections: Essays in Feminist Social Ethics* (Boston: Beacon Press, 1985), 135–51, and Suzanne Pharr, *Homophobia: A Weapon of Sexism* (Berkeley: Chardon Press, 1988).

33. The resources presented by Larry Graham are supportive of this approach to pastoral theology, care, and counseling. He suggests that there are five sources: "the actual practice of the ministry of care, . . . the social and cultural context . . . , the living religious tradition, . . . cognate secular knowledge, . . . and the personhood of the caretaker and pastoral theologian." See Larry K. Graham, *Care of Persons, Care of Worlds* (Nashville: Abingdon Press, 1992), 20–23.

34. This parallels the argument of John Patton in *From Ministry to Theology: Pastoral Action and Reflection* (Nashville: Abingdon Press, 1990).

35. See the classic work by William Clebsch and Charles Jaekle, *Pastoral Care in Historical Perspective* (New York: Jason Aronson, 1975). Ecclesial understandings directly shape the content and nature of pastoral care and counseling.

36. Don Browning has been most provocative in exploring the relationship between moral issues and pastoral care. See in particular his foundational work *The Moral Context of Pastoral Care* (Philadelphia: Westminster Press, 1976).

37. See Heyward, *Touching Our Strength*; Carter Heyward, *Staying Power: Reflections on Gender, Justice, and Compassion* (Cleveland: Pilgrim Press, 1995); and Nelson, *Embodiment*.

Chapter 2:
Claiming a Lesbian Identity
in the Context of Relationships

1. See the arguments found in Celia Kitzinger, *The Social Construction of Lesbianism* (London: SAGE Publications, 1987). For further discussion on the definition of lesbian identity, see Barbara Ponse, *Identities in the Lesbian World: The Social Construction of Self* (Westport, Conn.: Greenwood Press, 1978), 3–8. There are political struggles within the lesbian community about identity issues. Some women experience the pain of ostracism by other lesbians because they do not self-identify in public arenas or because they are not radical enough. The discussions by Kitzinger and Ponse illustrate some of these tensions.

2. For a detailed discussion of these terms, see Michael G. Shively and John P. De Cecco, "Components of Sexual Identity," in *Psychological Perspectives on Lesbian and Gay Male Experiences*, ed. Linda D. Garnets and Douglas C. Kimmel, 80–88 (New York: Columbia University Press, 1993); and Warren J. Blumenfeld and Diane Raymond, *Looking at Gay and Lesbian Life*, updated and expanded ed. (Boston: Beacon Press, 1988), 42–47.

3. Shively and De Cecco suggest that there is a difference between gender identity and social sex role. The former is more closely linked to the internal sense of being male or female that is being developed at a very early age. The idea of social sex role "refers to characteristics that are culturally associated with masculine or feminine . . . [and] largely tied to characteristics of appearance, behavior, and personality." Shively and De Cecco, "Components of Sexual Identity," 82. I have combined them into the notion of gender identity because of my conviction that external reality becomes internalized in the concrete embodiment of gender. External understandings are internalized in such a way as to suggest that the external and internal are intimately and intricately tied to each other.

4. For a discussion of the historical roots of the term women-identified women in the feminist movement, see Shane Phelan, *Identity Politics: Lesbian Feminism and the Limits of Community* (Philadelphia: Temple University Press, 1989), 37–58. In this book I will draw upon the work of radical lesbian feminists but will not be attending as much to their experiences in counseling. These are not women who, for the most part, will seek out the pastoral caregiver for assistance. Most radical women find the notion of therapy to be contrary to their understandings of what it means to be lesbians and whole persons who are empowered to heal in different ways. For further readings by radical lesbian feminists, see Celia Kitzinger and Rachel Perkins, *Changing Our Minds: Lesbian Feminism and Psychology* (New York: New York University Press, 1993); Phelan, *Identity Politics*; Ponse, *Identities in the Lesbian World*.

5. As De Cecco and Elia point out, "The idea of *sexual preference*, with its connotations of consciousness, intention, and choice occurring under unpredictable circumstances, is reduced to *sexual orientation*, a concept that asserts the presence of a single, fixed, independent biological mechanism that steers individual desire or behavior either toward men or toward women irrespective of circumstances and experience. As a reductionist concept, sexual orientation,

a biological given, transcends biography and history." John P. De Cecco and John P. Elia, "A Critique and Synthesis of Biological Essentialism and Social Constructionist Views of Sexuality and Gender," in *If You Seduce a Straight Person, Can You Make Them Gay? Issues in Biological Essentialism versus Social Constructionism in Gay and Lesbian Identities*, ed. John P. De Cecco and John P. Elia (New York: Haworth Press, 1993), 11. In utilizing the term *orientation identity* I do not want to suggest that there is not a conscious and intentional choice being made by women about their sexual preferences. I use the word *orientation*, however, because it most clearly indicates that being lesbian is not just sexual preference but how someone positions herself in the world.

6. Troiden notes that "[t]he homosexual identity is only one of several identities incorporated into a person's self-concept. . . . A perception of self as homosexual is an attitude, a potential line of action toward self and others, that is mobilized in settings (imagined or real) that are defined as sexual or romantic." Richard Troiden, "The Formation of Homosexual Identities," in *Psychological Perspectives on Lesbian and Gay Male Experiences*, ed. Linda D. Garnets and Douglas C. Kimmel (New York: Columbia University Press, 1993), 193. While I agree with Troiden's argument that the perception of homosexual identity is one piece of a more comprehensive identity, his dependence on the sexual or romantic experience distracts from the broader experience of many women's identity formation. Being lesbian has to do with more than just sexual relationships; it involves the way lesbians engage in the broader context of the world around them as well.

7. Beverly Greene, "Lesbian Women of Color: Triple Jeopardy," in *Women of Color: Integrating Ethnic and Gender Identities in Psychotherapy*, ed. Lillian Comas-Diaz and Beverly Greene (New York: Guilford Press, 1994), 389–427. For other resources, see Norma Garcia, Cheryl Kennedy, Sarah F. Pearlman, and Julia Perez, "The Impact of Race and Culture Differences: Challenges to Intimacy in Lesbian Relationships," in *Lesbian Psychologies: Explorations and Challenges*, ed. Boston Lesbian Psychologies Collective (Chicago: University of Illinois Press, 1987), 142–60; and the following articles in *Psychological Perspectives on Lesbian and Gay Male Experiences*, ed. Linda D. Garnets and Douglas C. Kimmel (New York: Columbia University Press, 1993): Connie S. Chan, "Issues of Identity Development among Asian-American Lesbians and Gay Men," 376–87; Oliva M. Espin, "Issues of Identity in the Psychology of Latina Lesbians," 348–63; Darryl K. Loiacano, "Gay Identity Issues among Black Americans: Racism, Homophobia, and the Need for Validation," 364–75; and Walter L. Williams, "Persistence and Change in the Berdache Tradition among Contemporary Lakota Indians," 339–47.

8. For a comprehensive review of the significance of names in the scriptures, see O. Odelain and R. Seguineau, *Dictionary of Proper Names and Places in the Bible*, trans. Matthew J. O'Connell (New York: Doubleday & Co., 1981).

9. Johannes B. Bauer notes that "[a]mong the Semites a name . . . is far from being a mere empty word. Rather it means something powerful, something that, the moment it is used, makes the person named present (1 Sam. 25:25): to know a person's name means to be able to exercise power over him [sic]." S.v. "Name," in *Sacramentum Verdi: An Encyclopedia of Biblical Theology*, vol. 2, ed. Johannes B. Bauer (New York: Herder & Herder, 1970), 611.

10. James B. Nelson and Sandra P. Longfellow, *Sexuality and the Sacred: Sources for Theological Reflection* (Louisville, Ky.: Westminster/John Knox Press, 1994), xiv. See also James B. Nelson, *Embodiment: An Approach to Sexuality and Christian Theology* (Minneapolis: Augsburg Publishing House, 1978), a classic text in sexual theology.

11. See Carter Heyward, *Touching Our Strength: The Erotic as Power and the Love of God* (San Francisco: Harper & Row, 1989); Audre Lorde, "Uses of the Erotic: The Erotic as Power," in *Sister Outsider* (Freedom, Calif.: Crossing Press, 1984), 53–59.

12. Heyward, *Touching Our Strength*, 99.

13. The concept of the image of God and its connection with lesbian and gay issues is currently under exploration by my colleague Larry Kent Graham. His construction of a pastoral theology gleaned from listening to the stories of lesbians and gay men illustrates how theology can be informed by the experiences of others.

14. Toinette M. Eugene, "While Love Is Unfashionable: Ethical Implications of Black Spirituality and Sexuality," in Nelson, *Sexuality and the Sacred*, 106.

15. Chris Glaser, *Coming Out to God: Prayers for Lesbians and Gay Men, Their Families and Friends* (Louisville, Ky.: Westminster/John Knox Press, 1991), 14.

16. See John J. McNeill, *Freedom, Glorious Freedom* (Boston: Beacon Press, 1995); Craig O'Neill and Kathleen Ritter, *Coming Out Within: Stages of Spiritual Awakening for Lesbians and Gay Men* (San Francisco: HarperCollins, 1992), 35–49.

17. Kathleen Ritter and Craig O'Neill, "Moving through Loss: The Spiritual Journey of Gay Men and Lesbian Women," *Journal of Counseling and Development* 68 (Sept/Oct 1989): 9.

18. Several texts note the importance of liberation. Two, in particular, talk about oppression and its manifestation in the forms of racism, classism, gender stereotyping, and other manifestations of bondage. See George R. Edwards, *Gay/Lesbian Liberation: A Biblical Perspective* (New York: Pilgrim Press, 1984); Gerre Goodman, George Lakey, Judy Lashof, and Erika Thorne, eds., *No Turning Back: Lesbian and Gay Liberation for the Eighties* (Philadelphia: New Society Publishers, 1983). Although both books come from the 1980s, they are instructive as they place the issues of lesbian liberation in historical perspective.

19. Dan Spencer, "Church at the Margins," in Nelson, *Sexuality and the Sacred*, 398.

20. For historical perspectives, see Lillian Faderman, *Odd Girls and Twilight Lovers: A History of Lesbian Life in Twentieth-Century America* (New York: Penguin Books, 1991); Jonathan Katz, *Gay American History: Lesbian and Gay Men in the U.S.A.* (New York: Thomas Y. Crowell Co., 1976).

21. Throughout this chapter I will be referring to psychodynamic theory, psychoanalytic literature, and psychotherapeutic methods in similar ways. These terms reflect very different and distinct theoretical perspectives. However, for purposes of this book it is helpful to think of them as a genre of literature, focusing on some of their commonalities, rather than as disparate theories that are not connected to one another. A number of persons are now writing about the

role of psychoanalytic theory in constructing perspectives on lesbian identity. In contemporary research much of the emphasis has centered on psychodynamic interpretations, most often relying upon a medical model of psychopathology and health. De Cecco and Elia suggest that there has been a shift in how science and medicine have been used in such endeavors. According to the authors, "The history of early modern northern Europe shows that a reconceptualization of gender occurred in the eighteenth century and a thorough medicalization of gender followed in the nineteenth century. . . . Under the panoply of science, it was medicine, in the nineteenth and twentieth centuries, that took over the popular view of sexuality and gender. In the nineteenth century it pathologized the two homosexual genders and the associated sexual behavior. In the twentieth century, medicine, now in the scientific garb of sexology, has attempted to quantify the older qualitative division of heterosexual vs. homosexual while retaining the notion of the heterosexual-homosexual dichotomy." De Cecco and Elia, "A Critique and Synthesis of Biological Essentialism," 3. For other notes about the historical development of psychodynamic literature, see Kenneth Lewes, *The Psychoanalytic Theory of Male Homosexuality* (New York: Simon & Schuster, 1988); Diane Richardson, "Recent Challenges to Traditional Assumptions about Homosexuality: Some Implications for Practice," in *Psychological Perspectives on Lesbian and Gay Male Experiences*, ed. Linda D. Garnets and Douglas C. Kimmel, 117–29 (New York: Columbia University Press, 1993).

22. Kristine L. Falco, *Psychotherapy with Lesbian Clients: Theory into Practice* (New York: Brunner/Mazel), 18.

23. The use of "psychoanalysts" is intentional here. Psychoanalysts are understood to be those persons who use traditional Freudian or neo-Freudian theory. Their therapy is highly structured and their theoretical orientations are clearly attached to traditional thought. Many psychotherapists draw upon psychoanalytic perspectives without becoming analysts.

24. S. Freud, "A Letter from Freud," *American Journal of Psychiatry* 107 (1950–1951): 107, 786–87, as quoted by Lewes, *Psychoanalytic Theory of Male Homosexuality*, 32. Freud was clear that homosexuality should not be understood as an illness nor should it be judged as a criminal act. According to Lewes, Freud signed the 1930 "public appeal to decriminalize homosexuality in Austria and Germany."

25. An adequate summary of the development of Freudian theoretical constructions for male homosexuality can be found in Lewes; Blumenfeld and Raymond, *Looking at Gay and Lesbian Life*, 133–38; George Weinberg, *Society and the Healthy Homosexual* (Garden City, N.Y.: Anchor Books, 1973).

26. For an expanded understanding of these theories within Freud's conceptual framework, see Lewes, *Psychoanalytic Theory of Male Homosexuality*, 35ff.; Weinberg, *Society and the Healthy Homosexual*, 21–25.

27. Weinberg, *Society and the Healthy Homosexual*, 24.

28. Ibid., 25.

29. Falco, citing in particular the work of Caprio, illustrates how the constructs outlined above appear in contemporary literature. Falco, *Psychotherapy with Lesbian Clients*, 22. Similarly, Blumenfeld and Raymond note that Helene Deutsch, a Freudian theorist, described lesbianism as being "unnatural." Her

reasoning fell along traditional lines and suggested that "there were two causes of lesbianism, one biological, the other *psychogenic* (meaning that some psychological complication has occurred that prevents 'normal' development). She cites narcissism as well as 'arrested development' (whereby the girl never outgrows her friendships with other girls), and the 'mother-relationship theory' (whereby the woman, realizing that she cannot have her mother, does not transfer her affections to her father but instead to other women)." Blumenfeld and Raymond, *Looking at Gay and Lesbian Life*, 136–37.

30. This theme has found its way into the literature, suggesting that women who have experienced sexual abuse choose to become lesbian because of their fear of, or hatred toward, men. This cannot be proven, since many women— both those who are heterosexual as well as those who are lesbian—can attest to the reality of being sexually abused in childhood. The sheer numbers of women in the world who have experienced abuse at the hands of men makes it probable that in a relationship consisting of two women the odds are higher than in a heterosexual relationship that one person in the relationship will be a sexual abuse survivor.

31. Lewes, *Psychoanalytic Theory of Male Homosexuality*, 47.

32. Vern Bullough, "The Kinsey Scale in Historical Perspective," in David P. McWhirter, Stephanie A. Sanders, and June Machover Reinisch, *Homosexuality/Heterosexuality: Concepts of Sexual Orientation* (New York: Oxford University Press, 1990), 3.

33. For an excellent review of Kinsey in the context of contemporary theory, see the collection of essays in McWhirter, Sanders, and Reinisch, *Homosexuality/Heterosexuality*.

34. Falco, *Psychotherapy with Lesbian Clients*, 23. In a similar vein is the work of Weinberg, who challenged other psychoanalysts and therapists about their views on homosexuality, encouraging them to think about how they might promote the development of a "healthy" homosexual. Weinberg, *Society and the Healthy Homosexual*.

35. Blumenfeld and Raymond, *Looking at Gay and Lesbian Life*, 138.

36. Ibid., 140.

37. Boston Lesbian Psychologies Collective, *Lesbian Psychologies*, 15.

38. See John Money, "Sin, Sickness, or Status? Homosexual Gender Identity and Psychoneuroendocrinology," in McWhirter, Sanders, and Reinisch, *Homosexuality/Heterosexuality*. For a critical review of this perspective, see Jay P. Paul, "Childhood Cross-Gender Behavior and Adult Homosexuality: The Resurgence of Biological Models of Sexuality," in De Cecco and Elia, "Critique and Synthesis," 41–54.

39. Much of the research on the biological or genetic link to homosexuality has been conducted with gay males. Illustrative of those who have offered critiques of essentialism from a variety of perspectives are Carter Heyward, *Touching Our Strength*, 37–47; Kitzinger, *Social Construction of Lesbianism*, 110–12; Diane Richardson, "The Dilemma of Essentiality in Homosexual Theory," *Journal of Homosexuality* 9 (1984): 79–90.

40. De Cecco and Elia, "Critique and Synthesis," 11.

41. Paul, "Childhood Cross-Gender Behavior," 41.

42. Linda D. Garnets and Douglas C. Kimmel, "Origins of Sexual Orientation," in Garnets and Kimmel, *Psychological Perspectives*, 112.

43. Thomas S. Weinberg, *Gay Men, Gay Selves: The Social Construction of Homosexual Identities* (New York: Irvington, 1983), 5.

44. Illustrative of this perspective is the work of Kitzinger and Perkins, *Changing Our Minds*.

45. For clarification of some of these issues, see Sue Vargo, "The Effects of Women's Socialization on Lesbian Couples," in Boston Lesbian Psychologies Collectives, *Lesbian Psychologies*, 161–73.

46. Vivienne Cass, "The Implications of Homosexual Identity Formation for the Kinsey Model and Scale of Sexual Preference," in McWhirter, Sanders, and Reinisch, *Homosexuality/Heterosexuality*, 250.

47. For a comparison with another model, see the work of Richard Troiden, "The Formation of Homosexual Identities," in Garnets and Kimmel, *Psychological Perspectives*, 191–217.

48. Cass, "Implications of Homosexual Identity Formation," 247.

49. Troiden, "Formation of Homosexual Identities," 194.

50. Troiden has suggested in his work on the development of homosexual identities that such stages be seen as suggestive of ideal types, or "heuristic devices, ways of organizing materials for analytical and comparative purposes, and are used as benchmarks against which one describes, compares, and tests hypotheses relating to empirical reality." Troiden, "Formation of Homosexual Identities," 194.

51. For further comment on this, see Cass, "Implications of Homosexual Identity Formation," 256.

52. For a description of Cass's stages, see Cass, "Implications of Homosexual Identity Formation," 248–51.

53. Troiden, "Formation of Homosexual Identities," 194. Herein lies partial explanation for the significant number of teens who attempt suicide because of their sexual orientation.

54. Cass, "Implications of Homosexual Identity Formation," 261.

55. Troiden, "Formation of Homosexual Identities," 202.

56. Richardson, "Dilemma of Essentiality," 122.

57. Troiden, "Formation of Homosexual Identities," 202–4.

58. Cass, "Implications of Homosexual Identity Formation," 248.

59. Troiden, "Formation of Homosexual Identities," 208–12.

Chapter 3:
Covenants of Love, Justice, and Mutuality

1. See John Boswell, *Same-Sex Unions in Premodern Europe* (New York: Villard Books, 1994); Gerda Lerner, *The Creation of Feminist Consciousness* (New York: Oxford University Press, 1993), and Gerda Lerner, *The Creation of Patriarchy* (New York: Oxford University Press, 1986). For a more traditional approach to the history of marriage, see Edward Westermarck, *A Short History of Marriage* (New York: Humanities Press, 1968).

2. Lerner, *Creation of Patriarchy*, 8.

3. Lerner's discussion of the stories of creation and the way that the Genesis accounts contribute to understandings of women as property of men are illuminating and troubling. See Lerner, *Creation of Patriarchy*, 180–98. Throughout Lerner's book she maintains, in part, that "sexual dominance underlies race and class dominance." Lerner, *Creation of Patriarchy*, 209. Lerner believes that patriarchy cannot be separated from the creation of the structures of marriage that legitimate male control over women's reproductive capacities.

4. In an articulate and persuasive essay, lawyer Paula Ettelbrick argues that legalizing lesbian and gay marriages would not necessarily mean that persons would find liberation, only that they might be "mainstreamed" into the cultural ideal of marriage in ways that are not helpful. See Ettelbrick, "Since When Is Marriage a Path to Liberation?" in *Lesbian and Gay Marriage: Private Commitments, Public Ceremonies*, ed. Suzanne Sherman (Philadelphia: Temple University Press, 1992), 20–26.

5. Lerner, *Creation of Patriarchy*, 214.

6. See Ettelbrick, "Since When Is Marriage a Path to Liberation?" and Mary Hunt, "You Do, I Don't," in *Open Hands* 6 (Fall 1990): 10–11.

7. Patricia Beattie Jung and Ralph F. Smith, *Heterosexism: An Ethical Challenge* (Albany: State University of New York Press, 1993), 140. Again, Lerner notes that in the biblical stories of creation in particular "the book of Genesis represented their [women's] definition as creatures essentially different from males; a redefinition of their sexuality as beneficial and redemptive only within the boundaries of patriarchal dominance; and finally the recognition that they were excluded from directly being able to represent the divine principle." Lerner, *Creation of Patriarchy*, 198. Also see Adrienne Rich's feminist classic, "Compulsory Heterosexuality and Lesbian Existence," in *The Lesbian and Gay Studies Reader*, ed. Henry Abelove, Michele Aina Barale, and David M. Halperin, 227–54 (New York: Routledge, 1993).

8. Tabor illustrates the way marriage participated in the legitimation and regulation of sexual behaviors, suggesting that "[t]he functions of marriage in the Old Testament are similar to those found for the majority of human societies." He outlines these functions as the regulation of sexual behavior (especially of women); economic functions; religious functions; and "most importantly, procreation, legitimation and socialization of children," 573. See Charles R. Taber, "Marriage," in *The Interpreter's Dictionary of the Bible*, Supplemental Volume (Nashville: Abingdon Press, 1976), 573–76.

9. Kath Weston, *Families We Choose: Lesbians, Gays, Kinship* (New York: Columbia University Press, 1991), 118. This study by Weston illustrates the breadth of lesbian and gay family structures. The topic of choice is addressed at length in chap. 5, "Families We Choose," 103–36.

10. Mary Hunt correctly notes that often the notion of marriage focuses on "coupledom" in ways that keep persons faced inward on the relationship rather than broadening their relationships to the community around them. See "You Do, I Don't," 10.

11. While I have contended that marriage is not an appropriate or helpful metaphor for talking about lesbian relationships, it is true that marriage is, in its most theologically construed sense, a covenant. Many theologians and litur-

gical resources explore the connection between marriage and covenant. See, for example, Paul W. Hoon, "The Order for the Service of Marriage," in *Companion to the Book of Worship*, ed. William F. Dunkle Jr. and Joseph D. Quillan Jr. (Nashville: Abingdon Press, 1970), 72–89; Paul F. Palmer, "Christian Marriage: Contract or Covenant?" in *Theological Studies* 33 (1972): 617–65. While Palmer confines his remarks to notions of heterosexual marriage within the Roman Catholic tradition, his article is helpful for thinking about covenant and its meaning in the context of significant relationships.

12. Palmer, "Christian Marriage," 619.

13. Ibid., 639.

14. See, for example, Klaus Baltzer, *The Covenant Formulary: Its Origin and Use in the Old Testament* (Philadelphia: Fortress Press, 1971); George Wesley Buchanan, *The Consequences of Covenant* (Leiden: E. J. Brill, 1970); Delbert R. Hillers, *Covenant: The History of a Biblical Idea* (Baltimore: Johns Hopkins Press, 1969). Hillers, in particular, summarizes many of the elements identified in this section on pages 176–77.

15. Hillers, *Covenant*, 176. Bernhard Anderson notes that one interpretation of the covenant with Moses indicates it was made by representatives who spoke on behalf of the community, while a second passage indicates that the covenant was established by direct action on the part of the members of the community. See, for example, the difference between Ex. 24:1–2, 9–11, and Ex. 24:3–8. Bernhard W. Anderson, *Understanding the Old Testament*, 3d ed. (Englewood Cliffs, N.J.: Prentice-Hall, 1975), 83–84.

16. Anderson, *Understanding the Old Testament*, 97. Anderson talks at length about covenant and its importance in the Hebrew scriptures and in the community of faith. In part, he highlights the difference between a suzerainty treaty (where a sovereign made covenant with people with less power) and a parity treaty (entered into mutually). The assumption made in this book is that lesbian partnerships should be formed clearly on the basis of shared power rather on positions of subordination and dominance. Hence, in utilizing the language of covenant I do not mean to imply in any way that the covenants established are done so out of the context of unequal balances of power. For an understanding of the differences in these covenants, see ibid., 88–91. My understanding parallels that found in process theology: covenants are formed on the basis of people co-creating relationship with God.

17. Hillers, *Covenant*, 177.

18. Walter Brueggemann, "The Covenanted Family: A Zone for Humanness," in *Journal of Current Social Issues* 14 (1977): 18–23.

19. Daniel Day Williams, *The Spirit and Forms of Love* (Lanham, Md.: University Press of America, 1981), 88. This text is insightful in its breadth and depth of historical considerations on the concept of love.

20. Mary E. Hunt, *Fierce Tenderness: A Feminist Theology of Friendship* (New York: Crossroad, 1991), 22.

21. Ibid., 100.

22. See Nancy Chodorow, *Feminism and Psychoanalytic Theory* (New Haven, Conn.: Yale University Press, 1989); Nancy Chodorow, *The Reproduction of Mothering: Psychoanalysis and the Sociology of Gender* (Berkeley: University of

California Press, 1978); Luise Eichenbaum and Susie Orbach, *Between Women* (New York: Viking Penguin, 1987); Luise Eichenbaum and Susie Orbach, *Understanding Women: A Feminist Psychoanalytic Perspective* (New York: Basic Books, 1983); Judith V. Jordan, Alexandra G. Kaplan, Jean Baker Miller, Irene P. Stiver, and Janet L. Surrey, *Women's Growth in Connection* (New York: Guilford Press, 1991).

23. See Chodorow, *Feminism and Psychoanalytic Theory*, Part I, "The Significance of Women's Mothering for Gender Personality and Gender Relation," 97–162.

24. See Eichenbaum and Orbach, *Between Women*, 51–52.

25. The differences between men and women in building relationships are a direct result of their internal developmental structures. As Eichenbaum and Orbach illustrate, men develop identities through their experiencing their difference from mothering figures, usually women. Women, on the other hand, develop their identities by being like the persons who mothered them. Hence, women tend to relate through their sense of attachment while men often relate through their differences. This becomes extremely significant in working with women in lesbian relationships since many refer to lesbian relationships as being enmeshed partnerships. This is an oversimplification of the processes and a minimizing of the importance of relationships for women. The most helpful analysis of this is in Eichenbaum and Orbach, *Between Women*.

26. Heyward, *Touching Our Strength*, 187.

27. See Philip Blumenstein and Pepper Schwartz, "Intimate Relationships and the Creation of Sexuality," in *Homosexuality/Heterosexuality: Concepts of Sexual Orientation*, ed. David P. McWhirter, Stephanie A. Sanders, and June Machover Reinisch, 307–20 (New York: Oxford University Press, 1990); Margaret Nichols, "Lesbian Relationships: Implications for the Study of Sexuality and Gender," in McWhirter, Sanders, and Reinisch, *Homosexuality/Heterosexuality*, 350–64.

28. Nichols, "Lesbian Relationships," 356–57. Carter Heyward notes in her definition of sexuality that embodied love is broader than genital sex. This is a significant point that cannot be overstated. Heyward, *Touching Our Strength*, 193, 194.

29. Blumenstein and Schwartz, "Intimate Relationships and the Creation of Sexuality," 315–16. These authors also contend that marriage as an institution directly affects the amount of sexual activity that happens between couples, both homosexual and heterosexual. When persons "marry" in the traditional and legal sense, they are less likely to have sex as frequently as when they were living together or living apart without the legal contract of marriage.

30. Virginia Ramey Mollenkott, *Sensuous Spirituality: Out from Fundamentalism* (New York: Crossroad, 1992), 98.

31. Williams, *Spirit and Forms of Love*, 14.

32. Pepper Schwartz, *Peer Marriage: How Love between Equals Really Works* (New York: Free Press, 1994), 45.

33. Larry K. Graham, *Care of Persons, Care of Worlds* (Nashville: Abingdon Press, 1992), 44.

34. See, for example, Graham, *Care of Persons;* Heyward, *Touching Our Strength;* Hunt, *Fierce Tenderness;* Mollenkott, *Sensuous Spirituality;* James B. Nelson, *Embodiment: An Approach to Sexuality and Christian Theology* (Minneapolis: Augsburg Publishing House, 1978); James N. Poling, *The Abuse of Power: A Theological Problem* (Nashville: Abingdon Press, 1991).

35. For an excellent examination of distinctive perspectives on justice, see Karen Lebacqz, *Six Theories of Justice: Perspectives from Philosophical and Theological Ethics* (Minneapolis: Augsburg Publishing House, 1986).

36. Graham, *Care of Persons,* 44.

37. Ibid.

38. Schwartz, *Peer Marriages,* 46–54.

39. Hunt, *Fierce Tenderness,* 101.

40. In her work on sexual ethics Carter Heyward notes that there are seven qualities of right relatedness, which include: "courage, compassion, anger, forgiveness, touching, healing, faith." These characteristics are inherent in covenantal partnerships and can be used as benchmarks for women as they negotiate the conflicts present in their relationships. See Heyward, *Touching Our Strength,* 139.

41. Jean Baker Miller, *Women and Power* (working paper; Stone Center for Developmental Services and Studies; Wellesley, Mass.: Wellesley College, 1982).

42. Schwartz, *Peer Marriage,* 48.

43. Graham, *Care of Persons,* 44.

44. Heyward, *Touching Our Strength,* 191.

45. Jung and Smith, *Heterosexism,* 161.

46. Elizabeth Kassoff, "Nonmonogamy in the Lesbian Community," in *Women and Therapy: A Feminist Quarterly* 8 (1989): 167.

47. Jung and Smith, *Heterosexism,* 150.

48. Lerner notes that marriages and partnerships were formed around issues of economic ownership. Hence, monogamy became a way of marking one's direct connection and link to the creation of children. Women were important pieces of property who had to be protected from others. Lerner, *Creation of Patriarchy.*

49. J. Michael Clark, *A Defiant Celebration: Theological Ethics and Gay Sexuality* (Garland, Tex.: Tangelwuld Press, 1990), 40. In this book Clark presents one of the most balanced examinations of the issue of monogamy from the perspective of emerging sexual ethics for gay men and lesbians. As he notes, "we are more free, as gay men and lesbians, to critically evaluate relationship patterns and to choose whether we will engage in or make commitments to monogamous or nonmonogamous relationships." Clark, *Defiant Celebration,* 35–36.

50. Heyward, *Touching Our Strength,* 137.

51. Kassoff, "Nonmonogamy in the Lesbian Community."

52. Betty Berzon, *Permanent Partners: Building Gay and Lesbian Relationships That Last* (New York: E. P. Dutton, 1988), 10–15.

53. D. Merilee Clunis and G. Dorsey Green, *Lesbian Couples* (Seattle: Seal Press, 1988). For a similar developmental structure based on research with

male couples, see David P. McWhirter and Andrew M. Mattison, *The Male Couple: How Relationships Develop* (Englewood Cliffs, N.J.: Prentice-Hall, 1984). Their model consists of six stages as well: blending, nesting, maintaining, building, releasing, and renewing.

54. These stages are articulated in Clunis and Green, *Lesbian Couples*, 10–28.

55. Ibid., 14.

56. Ibid., 16.

57. Ibid., 20.

58. Ibid., 22.

59. Ibid., 25.

60. Ibid., 27.

61. Ibid., 28.

62. Jung and Smith, *Heterosexism*, 162–63.

Chapter 4:
Challenges to Covenantal Partnerships

1. See Ellen F. Ratner, "Treatment Issues for Chemically Dependent Lesbians and Gay Men," in *Psychological Perspectives on Lesbian and Gay Male Experiences*, ed. Linda D. Garnets and Douglas C. Kimmel, 567–78 (New York: Columbia University Press, 1993).

2. See Robert J. Kus, "Alcoholism and Non-Acceptance of Gay Self: The Critical Link," *Journal of Homosexuality* 15 (1988): 25–42.

3. There are many who debate the bars' contributions to the high incidence of alcoholism among the gay and lesbian population. Kus, for example, suggests that the high incidence of alcoholism is not related to gay bars. Others argue that gay bars are significant contributing factors to high incidences of alcoholism. For a contrasting view, see Carl Douglas, *Counseling Same-Sex Couples* (New York: W. W. Norton & Co., 1990), 137; Kus, "Alcoholism and Non-Acceptance," 38.

4. See Dusty Miller, "Women in Pain: Substance Abuse/Self-Medication," in *The Social and Political Contexts of Family Therapy*, ed. Marsha Pravder Mirkin, 179–92 (Boston: Allyn & Bacon, 1990).

5. See Ratner, "Treatment Issues," 570.

6. JoAnn Loulan, *Lesbian Sex* (San Francisco: Spinsters/aunt lute, 1984), 180. Loulan lists the difficulties for women, including less ability to achieve orgasm in early stages of sobriety.

7. Ratner, "Treatment Issues," 574.

8. Loulan, *Lesbian Sex*, 190.

9. Patricia I. Zibung Huffman, "Recovery as a Necessary Precursor to Effective Therapy," in *Gays, Lesbians, and Their Therapists*, ed. Charles Silverstein (New York: W. W. Norton & Co., 1991), 104.

10. In popular therapeutic terms this gets at the complexity of co-dependency. I choose not to use this term because it reflects negative images of caregiving. Instead, what is important for working with women in lesbian partnerships is to affirm their presence to each other and to encourage them to become more mutual

in that process rather than focused only on one person. For a perspective on co-dependency, see Sondra Smalley, "Dependency Issues in Lesbian Relationship," *Journal of Homosexuality* 14 (1987): 125–35.

11. Kus, "Alcoholism and Non-Acceptance of Gay Self," 39.

12. For those who have been more connected to the lesbian bar scene than appears to be the case for Peggy and Sherry, twelve-step groups can provide a way of developing social relationships that are drug-free. This, in and of itself, can be important in the process of recovery for many lesbians. See Kristine L. Falco, *Psychotherapy with Lesbian Clients: Theory into Practice* (New York: Brunner/Mazel), 151.

13. Rochelle L. Klinger, "Treatment of a Lesbian Batterer," in Silverstein, *Gays, Lesbians and Their Therapists,* 132. Good resources on lesbian battering are available in many local bookstores. See Sharon Smith Daughtery, *Closeted Screams: A Service Provider Handbook for Same-Sex Domestic Violence Issues* (Denver: Smith-Fleisen Sorian Publishing, 1992); Kerry Lobel, ed., *Naming the Violence: Speaking Out about Lesbian Battering* (Seattle: Seal Press, 1986); Claire M. Renzetti, *Violent Betrayal: Partner Abuse in Lesbian Relationships* (Newbury Park, Calif.: Sage, 1992).

14. According to one study, 25 percent of women in lesbian partnerships have experienced physical abuse. Other studies suggest that this figure may be lower—actually 10 to 15 percent of women are in lesbian battering situations. At any rate, lesbian battering is common in too many lesbian partnerships. Studies cited in Klinger, "Treatment of a Lesbian Batterer," 126–42.

15. Ibid., 134.

16. Huffman suggests, along with others, that at least 25 percent of women have experienced some form of traumatic sexual abuse in their history. See Huffman, "Recovery as a Necessary Precursor to Effective Therapy."

17. For limited, but helpful, resources, see Ellen Bass and Laura Davis, *The Courage to Heal: A Guide for Women Survivors of Sexual Abuse* (New York: Harper & Row, 1988); Laura Davis, *Allies in Healing* (New York: HarperCollins, 1991).

18. For a set of exercises to use with lesbian partners, see Loulan, *Lesbian Sex,* 271.

19. Ibid., 270.

20. Ibid., 271.

21. Thelma Goodrich, Barbara Ellman, Cheryl Rampage, and Kris Halstead, "The Lesbian Couple," in Mirkin, *The Social and Political Contexts of Family Therapy,* 168. For an alternative to systems theory, see Valory Mitchell, "Using Kohut's Self Psychology in Work with Lesbian Couples," *Women and Therapy* 8, no. 1/2 (1988): 157–66.

22. Julie Mencher, "Intimacy in Lesbian Relationships: A Critical Re-Examination of Fusion," *Work in Progress* (Wellesley, Mass.: Wellesley College, 1990), 7.

23. Sallyann Roth, "Psychotherapy with Lesbian Couples: Individual Issues, Female Socialization and the Social Context," *Journal of Marital and Family Therapy* 11, no. 3 (1985): 275.

24. Jo-Ann Krestan and Claudia Bepko, "The Problem of Fusion in the Lesbian Relationship," *Family Process* 19 (1980): 278.

25. Mencher, "Intimacy in Lesbian Relationships," 4.
26. Ibid., 9.

Chapter 5:
Maintaining and Extending Families

1. Ray S. Anderson and Dennis B. Guernsey, *On Being Family: A Social Theology of the Family* (Grand Rapids: Wm. B. Eerdmans Publishing Co., 1985), 14.

2. For an interesting list of definitions of family, see J. Ann Craig and Linda S. Elmiger, eds., *Family: Drawing the Circle Wide* (New York: Women's Division, 1994), 150–51. This United Methodist Women's study book is helpful in addressing some of the complexities of defining "family" from various perspectives.

3. There are many good pastoral counseling books on families. For the most part these are limited to traditional heterosexual couples, intergenerational families, and normative understandings of blended families. However, they provide meaningful insights into issues articulated in this chapter. The texts I find most helpful are: Herb Anderson, *The Family and Pastoral Care* (Philadelphia: Fortress Press, 1984); Edwin H. Friedman, *Generation to Generation: Family Process in Church and Synagogue* (New York: Guilford Press, 1985); John Patton and Brian H. Childs, *Christian Marriage and Family: Caring for Our Generations* (Nashville: Abingdon Press, 1988); J. C. Wynn, *Family Therapy in Pastoral Ministry*, rev. and expanded ed. (San Francisco: HarperCollins, 1991).

4. Patton and Childs, *Christian Marriage and Family*, 130.

5. For an excellent perspective on the diversity of families in scripture, see the listing included in Virginia Ramey Mollenkott, *Sensuous Spirituality: Out from Fundamentalism* (New York: Crossroad, 1993), 194–97.

6. For a discussion of idolatry and traditional family perceptions in the context of church, see Janet Fishburn, *Confronting the Idolatry of Family: A New Vision for the Household of God* (Nashville: Abingdon Press, 1991).

7. Anderson, *The Family and Pastoral Care*, 69.

8. See in particular Patton and Childs, introduction and chap. 1: "Creatures Who Care," in *Christian Marriage and Family*, 11–44.

9. I am indebted to the work of Heyward in identifying coming out as a "relational process." See Carter Heyward, *Touching Our Strength: The Erotic as Power and the Love of God* (San Francisco: Harper & Row, 1989), 21.

10. Heyward, *Touching Our Strength*, 24.

11. Patricia Beattie Jung and Ralph F. Smith, *Heterosexism: An Ethical Challenge* (Albany: State University of New York Press, 1993), 171.

12. For an insightful discussion of passing, see Barbara Ponse, *Identities in the Lesbian World: The Social Construction of Self* (Westport, Conn.: Greenwood Press, 1978), 59–63. Ponse's comments are particularly instructive when considering the social dynamics of constructing identity and the role of external validation in that process.

13. Jung and Smith, *Heterosexism*, 178.

14. Erik F. Strommen, "You're a What? Family Members' Reactions to the Disclosure of Homosexuality," in *Psychological Perspectives on Lesbian and Gay Male Experiences*, ed. Linda D. Garnets and Douglas C. Kimmel (New York: Columbia University Press, 1993), 249.

15. Jung and Smith, *Heterosexism*, 178.

16. For an interesting set of articles on outing and its psychodynamic and political ramifications, see *Journal of Homosexuality* 27, no. 3/4 (1994): 27–110.

17. Nanette Gartrell, "Issues in Psychotherapy with Lesbian Women," *Work in Progress* (Wellesley, Mass: Wellesley College, 1984), 6. Gartrell is one of the strongest proponents for the argument that lesbians need lesbian therapists who are "out" and not closeted. Without such openness, she believes it is impossible for women in lesbian partnerships to receive adequate care and counseling.

18. For a more complete argument, see Gartrell, "Issues in Psychotherapy with Lesbian Women."

19. Ponse, *Identities in the Lesbian World*, 86.

20. Gartrell, "Issues in Psychotherapy with Lesbian Women," 7.

21. Jung and Smith, *Heterosexism*, 174–75.

22. Sherry Zitter, "Coming Out to Mom: Theoretical Aspects of the Mother-Daughter Process," in *Lesbian Psychologies: Explorations and Challenges*, ed. Boston Lesbian Psychologies Collective (Chicago: University of Illinois Press, 1987), 189.

23. Kath Weston, *Families We Choose: Lesbians, Gays, Kinship* (New York: Columbia University Press, 1991), 67.

24. I am indebted to Larry Graham for his guidance on this issue during a conversation about the writing of this book.

25. Jung and Smith, *Heterosexism*, 176–78.

26. Heyward, *Touching Our Strength*, 28.

27. Jung and Smith, *Heterosexism*, 177.

28. For an insightful first-hand account of one woman's journey of coming out publicly and having that experience serve as a catalyst for others, see Mary Gaddis, "The Joys of Being Out," *Open Hands* 5, no. 1 (Sept 1989): 12. There are many such stories and accounts. Perhaps one of the best known is that found in Chris Glaser, *Uncommon Calling: A Gay Man's Struggle to Serve the Church* (San Francisco: Harper & Row, 1988).

29. J. Michael Clark, *A Place to Start* (Dallas: Monument Press, 1989), 125.

30. Ibid., 124.

31. There is a growing body of literature on coming out in the context of families. Some of the most helpful aimed at parents includes: Mary V. Borhek, *Coming Out to Parents: A Two-Way Survival Guide for Lesbians and Gay Men and Their Parents* (New York: Pilgrim Press, 1983); Carolyn Welch Griffin, Marian J. Wirth, and Arthur G. Wirth, *Beyond Acceptance: Parents of Lesbians and Gays Talk about Their Experiences* (Englewood Cliffs, N.J.: Prentice-Hall, 1986); David K. Switzer and Shirley Switzer, *The Parents of the Homosexual* (Philadelphia: Westminster Press, 1980). One of the best resources for parents is the literature produced by the Parents and Friends of Lesbians and Gay (PFLAG), which has local chapters in many cities.

32. Craig O'Neill and Kathleen Ritter, *Coming Out Within: Stages of Spiritual Awakening for Lesbians and Gay Men* (San Francisco: HarperCollins, 1992). This book offers a powerful perspective of the process of moving from loss to transformation.

33. This process is talked about in a number of sources. See, for example, Borhek, *Coming Out to Parents*, 21–30; O'Neill and Ritter, *Coming Out Within*, 7–12; Strommen, "Family Members' Reaction," 252; Zitter, "Coming Out to Mom," 184.

34. Borhek, *Coming Out to Parents*, 22.

35. Ibid., 23.

36. O'Neill and Ritter, *Coming Out Within*, 8.

37. Strommen, "Family Members' Reactions," 253.

38. Weston, *Families We Choose*, 52.

39. Ibid., 52–56.

40. Zitter, "Coming Out to Mom," 177–94.

41. Ibid., 185.

42. Strommen, "Family Members' Reactions," 250.

43. Christine Browning, Amy L. Reynolds, and Sari H. Dworkin, "Affirmative Psychotherapy for Lesbian Women," *The Counseling Psychologist* 19, no. 2 (April 1991): 179.

44. Weston, *Families We Choose*, 64.

45. Strommen, "Family Members' Reactions," 259.

46. These stages are outlined in Strommen, "Family Members' Reactions," 251.

47. Ibid., 251.

48. For stories of two mothers' journeys in relationship to their gay sons, see Borhek, *Coming Out to Parents*; Agnes G. Herman, "A Parent's Journey Out of the Closet," in *Twice Blessed: On Being Lesbian or Gay and Jewish*, ed. Christie Balka and Andy Rose, 118–25 (Boston: Beacon Press, 1989).

49. Ellen Lewin, *Lesbian Mothers: Accounts of Gender in American Culture* (Ithaca, N.Y.: Cornell University Press, 1993), 46.

50. Strommen, "Family Members' Reactions," 257.

51. Ibid., 257–61. Strommen notes that an under-researched area in homosexuality studies is that of the responses of women who have been in heterosexual marriages and their children.

52. A study by Bell and Weinberg "indicated that between one-third and one-half of all lesbians were married at one time and that approximately 50 percent of these marriages produced children." Kristine L. Falco, *Psychotherapy with Lesbian Clients: Theory into Practice* (New York: Brunner/ Mazel, 1991), 127, quoting from a study by A. P. Bell and M. S. Weinberg, *Homosexualities: A Study of Diversity among Men and Women* (New York: Touchstone, 1978).

53. D. Merilee Clunis and G. Dorsey Green, *Lesbian Couples* (Seattle: Seal Press, 1988), 112. A recent and helpful book that explores lesbian motherhood is Phyllis Burke, *Family Values: Two Moms and Their Sons* (New York: Random House, 1993).

54. Lewin, *Lesbian Mothers*, 182.

55. Sally Crawford, "Lesbian Families: Psychosocial Stress and the Family-Building Process," in *Lesbian Psychologies: Explorations and Challenges*, ed. Boston Lesbian Psychologies Collective (Chicago: University of Illinois Press, 1987), 200.

56. Crawford, "Lesbian Families," 199.

57. Clunis and Green, *Lesbian Couples*, 126.

58. Crawford, "Lesbian Families," 195.

59. For an excellent commentary on some of this research, see Patricia J. Falk, "Lesbian Mothers: Psychosocial Assumptions in Family Law," in Garnets and Kimmel, *Psychological Perspectives*, 420–36. Falk is extremely articulate on the legal arguments that have been used against lesbian mothers in custody hearings and legal battles.

60. Falk, "Lesbian Mothers," 431.

61. Crawford, "Lesbian Families," 201–3.

62. Weston, *Families We Choose*, 212.

63. Falk, "Lesbian Mothers," 422. See also Lewin, *Lesbian Mothers*, 64ff.

64. Clunis and Green, *Lesbian Couples*, 116.

65. Bernice Goodman, "Lesbian Mothers," in *Keys to Caring: Assisting Your Gay and Lesbian Clients*, ed. Robert J. Kus, 119–24 (Boston: Alyson Publications, 1990).

66. Crawford, "Lesbian Families," 196.

67. Weston, *Families We Choose*, 165.

68. For an expanded discussion of these choices, see Lewin, *Lesbian Mothers*, 46–74.

69. Joanna Bunker Rohrbaugh, "Choosing Children: Psychological Issues in Lesbian Parenting," *Women and Therapy* 8, no. 1/2 (1988): 54. For a fuller discussion of issues surrounding choices between adoption and biological childbirth see this complete article, pp. 51–64.

70. Crawford, "Lesbian Families," 205.

71. Weston, *Families We Choose*, 33.

72. Judith Plaskow, "Toward a New Theology of Sexuality," in Balka and Rose, *Twice Blessed*, 151.

73. Weston, *Families We Choose*, 107.

74. Jo-Ann Krestan and Claudia Bepko, "The Problem of Fusion in the Lesbian Relationship," *Family Process* 19, no. 3 (Sept 1980): 280.

75. Weston, *Families We Choose*, 117.

76. Ibid., 212.

Chapter 6:
Pastoral Theology and Community

1. J. R. Burck, "Community, Fellowship, and Care," in *The Dictionary of Pastoral Care and Counseling*, ed. Rodney Hunter (Nashville: Abingdon Press, 1990), 202–3.

2. For a powerful message on communities and their importance in the spiritual lives of lesbians and gay men, see Chris Glaser, *Coming Out to God:*

Prayers for Lesbians and Gay Men, Their Families and Friends (Louisville, Ky.: Westminster/John Knox Press, 1991), 75–116.

3. Dan Spencer, "Church at the Margins," *Christianity and Crisis* 52, no. 8 (May 25, 1992): 174–76.

4. For illustrations of this, see J. Michael Clark, *A Place to Start* (Dallas: Monument Press, 1989), 175–79; Valerie DeMarinis, *Critical Caring: A Feminist Model for Pastoral Psychology* (Louisville, Ky.: Westminster/John Knox Press, 1993), 121–44.

5. Kristine L. Falco, *Psychotherapy with Lesbian Clients: Theory into Practice* (New York: Brunner/Mazel, 1991), 43–45.

6. Nanette Gartrell, "Issues in Psychotherapy with Lesbian Women," *Works in Progress* (Wellesley, Mass.: Wellesley College, 1984), 28.

Index

Printed in the United States
45655LVS00008B/244-264